HAUNTED
VANCOUVER,
WASHINGTON

HAUNTED VANCOUVER, WASHINGTON

PAT JOLLOTA

Published by Haunted America
A Division of The History Press
Charleston, SC
www.historypress.com

Cover: The House of Providence, known as the academy, was built in 1873 by Mother Joseph of the Sacred Heart. It was the largest brick building north of San Francisco. Mother Joseph went on to build twenty-nine more schools and hospitals. She died in 1902, and her grave site is a National Historic Site. A statue of Mother Joseph represents Washington State in Statuary Hall in our nation's capital. *Author's collection.*

First published 2020

Manufactured in the United States

ISBN 9781467145510

Library of Congress Control Number: 2020934367

CONTENTS

Preface

It seems unlikely that someone who has never seen or heard a ghost would become the custodian of so many stories about them. But there I was, for more than twenty years, behind the desk marked "curator" at the Clark County Historical Museum in Vancouver, Washington.

One of our services was to assist clients as they researched their property. Most of the time, it was mundane. There would be developers doing an environmental impact study or someone researching for historic register designation. Sometimes, it's simply people curious about those who lived in the house before them. Once in a great while, honestly, it was about who they could sue.

Then there were the others—the ones who were slightly evasive, somewhat diffident about just what it was they were looking for. The aerial photo collection did not interest them. No, fire insurance maps just didn't fit the bill. City directories seemed to pique a bit of interest but not much.

"What is it exactly that you're hoping to find?"

Now the answer came out—sometimes with an air of bravado. The chin lifts up, the lips tighten. "You'll think that I'm crazy, but I think the place is haunted."

Oh, another one. The search shifted from the dirt and bricks and timber to the people who lived or worked at the property. Who were they? What were their stories? We were looking for names, old cemetery records, old directories and vintage newspapers.

If all went well, we would find a tragedy in the house or, better yet, a violent crime. They would go away happy. Their story was justified. They weren't crazy or thought to be foolish. They could now tell their stories with references.

Of course, if a house is old enough, there will be a tragedy. Humans dwelled in those structures.

I was in the ideal place to collect these stories. Like a gray-haired spider, I waited, and the stories came to me. I just gathered them. These stories fascinated me. I began to tell them to others. That would encourage more people to share their own experiences. Some of these events happened only once. Some of them have been repeated events—the tales told and retold. All are valid.

Are these stories true? The people who told me of their experiences most decidedly believed them, and I believed the tellers. The reports of tragedy, violence and fear are definitely true. They leap from the brittle pages of old newspapers.

The stories remind us again and again that there is nothing new in our society. The narratives of long ago could be those on the pages of our newspapers today. The tales are of revenge, jealousy, hatred, lingering remorse, guilt and regret. There is nothing new.

Here, then, are the stories that I've heard and noted over many years.

ACKNOWLEDGEMENTS

No work such as this can be done by a writer alone. It's imperative that stories, resources and opinions be shared.

While acknowledgements usually end with "the great librarians at," I want to start with the great librarians on the fourth floor of the downtown Fort Vancouver Regional Library. They're always there, from pointing out recent reference acquisitions of interest to starting a recalcitrant microfilm reader to just offering support. The library designers scored a solid win by placing the librarian desk right in the middle of the room instead of barricaded behind a counter. Thank you, one and all.

An incredible amount of encouragement and handholding was done by my incredible editor, Laurie Krill.

Voices from the past were heard in old notes from my curator days: former directors Gus Norwood and David Freece and colleagues Bill Alley, Doug Magedanz, Victoria Ransom, Bradley Richardson and Gretchen Hoyt.

Friends or witnesses include Traci Meyer-Jones, Doug Luse, Royce Pollard, Beth Hovee, Hunter Cavilee, Holly Chamberlain, Lynette Blackard, Tara Lundy, Randy Brasmer, Dan Wyatt, Marcell Gareis, Arden Williams, Finch Corine Tiffany, Annette Emerson and Leah Jackson.

The oldest city in Washington State, Vancouver sprawls along the Columbia River. It's joined to Portland, Oregon, by two traffic bridges and a railroad bridge. *Author's collection.*

INTRODUCTION

Vancouver, Washington, is the oldest city in the state. It grew on the banks of the mighty Columbia River. Writers at the National Historic Site refer to this area as "One Place Across Time." That is an apt title. This little corner of the state saw the Chinook Nation's grandest era, Captain William Broughton's exploration in 1792 and then the Lewis and Clark Corps of Discovery sailed past in 1805 and 1806. In 1824, the Hudson's Bay Company set up shop at the confluence of the Columbia and the Willamette. As the Hudson's Bay grew, the Oregon Trail branched off to end at the fort for supplies. In 1846, the treaty was signed that made Washington a part of the United States, and the United States Army arrived in 1849 to create what is now the oldest American military installation in the Pacific Northwest. From this base, soldiers marched to the Civil War, the Spanish American War, two world wars, Korea, Vietnam and the conflicts of today. The oldest operating airfield in the United States is here, which brought balloon flights in 1911, airmail service in the post–World War I era, the Chkalov flight and the first transpolar flight in 1937. Mighty shipyards rose and disappeared during both world wars. All of this and more happened in the same few hundred acres along the river. One place across time, indeed.

While all of this was happening, a town was growing, and people carried on their businesses, romances, tragedies, successes and failures. From this rich tapestry grew the stories that we tell.

1
DOWNTOWN

Interstate Bridge

The Interstate Bridge crosses the Columbia River between Vancouver, Washington and Portland, Oregon. The span that is now the northbound span was the first built and opened in 1917. Then it was a two-way route with a streetcar line down the center. Today, freeway traffic thunders across. There is a walkway on the north side of the span. On that walkway, a tall, slender man has been seen. He wears an overcoat and a fedora hat.

Some people driving on that bridge have seen him on misty evenings. They sense that he is in some sort of trouble and want to help him. But when they look in their mirrors, he is gone. A woman, giving her name only as Johanna, said that she had actually met the ghost as she walked across the bridge one night. He didn't seem to see here, nor did he return her greeting. When she turned around to look back, he was gone.

There is a hump in the bridge. It's not original. When the second span across the river was built, it had a hump to allow ships to sail under to decrease the number of bridge lifts. When that bridge opened, the first was rebuilt to have a matching hump. That's where the man disappears. He walks into the hump and vanishes.

There have been many tragedies on the bridge, including car crashes and suicides. During a July 4 water show in 1934, the second Columbia Regatta, a young daredevil, Roland McCall, was killed when he dove 110 feet from the top of the bridge into the river. His body was not found until

When Mayor Percival walked across the Interstate Bridge, it was a flat, single span structure with walkways on either side. *Author's collection.*

August 21. None of those accounts, however, fit the tale told by those who have seen the figure. Only one story matched, and that was the account of Mayor Grover Percival.

The mayor walked onto the bridge on election night, October 17, 1920, and never returned. A search was undertaken, but it would be a month before his body was found on Hayden Island. He was hanging in a tree—hanged with his own handkerchief.

There seemed to be no reason for the suicide. His health was not good, but he was still active. He was in no financial trouble. He was not in political trouble; in fact, he was not running for reelection that night. His good friend John P. Kiggins won the race that evening.

What could have been going through his mind as he smiled, tipped his hat to the ladies and set out across the bridge? What despair accompanied him as he greeted his friends as he passed? Why does he cross the bridge again and again? Would he undo that dreadful night? Or could it be that it was not a suicide but a murder? Hanging oneself with a handkerchief seems implausible.

He had been instrumental in getting the bridge built two years before. It had been controversial, and there were lawsuits to try to stop it. The

Governor had vetoed the funding for it. The two counties, Multnomah in Oregon and Clark in Washington, had raised the money for the bridge through loans and raised taxes. Feelings had run high.

We will never know the true story.

LOST AIRMAN

A bartender in Warehouse 23, a restaurant by the bridge, spoke of screams in the night—a scream that echoed. It was a scream of horror and agony. He had been closing the restaurant. He locked up quickly and fled. What could have caused that sound?

People from Camas to Swan Island used to talk of a lost airplane. Planes are so common today that no one notices an airplane overhead unless it's very low. Can these two phenomena be related? Perhaps.

It was very foggy on a November night in 1928. It was so foggy that Clarence Price could not find the Portland Airport, a new airport on Swan Island. He flew up and down the river—often at just fifty feet above the water. People in Camas heard him. A mechanic at Swan Island heard him and sent up a flare. The pilot must not have seen the flare. He flew east to

Curious spectators and souvenir-seekers crowd around Clarence Price's shattered mail plane. *Author's collection.*

Camas and circled. He flew past Pearson Field, was a military field then used by the 321st Observation Squadron. Mail planes had landed there before Swan Island.

He'd been a pilot in World War I, which is when he learned to fly. He'd flown mail for Varney Aviation since 1926. When he was once more to Camas, he banked back, flying very low and hoping to see something on the ground.

Ahead was the Interstate Bridge. He must have thought he was well above it. But the lift span with its giant counterweights, great concrete blocks, rose 110 feet. Price's plane hit one of the towers and spiraled into the lumberyard below. It burst into flames. Townspeople rushed to both help the pilot and to grab bits of the plane as souvenirs.

He never regained consciousness and died soon after. Is it his scream that was heard in the night as the great bulk of a steel bridge appeared out of the fog? The place where the plane hit would be west of the kitchen of today's restaurant. Listen on a foggy night, and you might hear the motor of the little plane flying east and west, searching.

A strange side note: a bit of mail from the crash was sent to a Portland newspaper. It was a scorched photograph of a four-engine Fokker that had crashed into a house in Long Island the week before.

ROOM 160

Across the lobby of the Thunderbird Inn at the Quay, a doorway opened into a hallway. You could walk all the way to the back of the hotel, where a corridor crossed. Turn right and walk to the door of room 160. The woman in room 160 has been one of the most reported hauntings in Vancouver.

The first was from a housekeeper in the hotel. She had been checking empty rooms to make sure that they would be ready to rent. She opened the door of room 160, and a woman was sitting on the bed. "Oh, I'm so sorry!" she said as she backed out of the room. She immediately reopened the door to see if the woman needed anything. The room was empty.

One night there was an ice storm. Management at the hotel told staff to not try driving home but to pick rooms and stay the night. No one wanted room 160.

The next report was from a tourist couple from California. The husband awoke in the night to see a figure standing at the foot of the bed. He caught a glimpse of a glittery garment. He quickly turned on the bedside lamp to,

The Inn at the Quay Hotel stretched along the Port's Berth One just west of the bridge. The restaurant had been the City Prune Warehouse. *Author's collection.*

you guessed it, nothing. At breakfast the next morning, he mentioned the episode to the waiter.

"Ah," said the waiter. "You must be in room 160. There was a murder there."

The couple headed straight for the museum and told their story. Research revealed a shocking tale. Jackie Charles Patterson was an appealing little man with a crooked smile. He walked with a limp. His family later testified that he'd been deprived of oxygen at birth, so he did illogical things.

He and his wife, Marcia, had a most unusual marriage. She lived in Vancouver in McLoughlin Heights. He lived in Arizona. When he wanted to see her, he'd tear a $100 bill in half and send half to her. If she wanted the other half, she'd have to see him.

The marriage was over, and Marcia decided to file for divorce. In response, he sent her halves of five $100 bills. A meeting was set up. She dressed in her best and put on a wig. Wigs were fashionable in 1975.

Patterson took the train to Vancouver and bought a used car downtown. His next stop was the Fort Motel. He rented a room and then almost immediately checked out. At the Thunderbird Inn at the Quay, he found what he wanted: a room far off the road, at the back, by the parking lot—room 160. He set off to pick up Marcia.

They dined at a downtown restaurant, Onslow's, where the waitstaff described them as friendly to each other. At the hotel, however, the mood changed. They argued, perhaps over the divorce. He put a pillow over her chest and fired two bullets into her heart.

Since Patterson was the only one who walked out of that room, we must take his word for what happened nest. He carried his wife, wrapped in the bedspread, out of the room, down the hall and out to his car, where he placed her in the trunk. He went back for the wig, put it in the hotel wastebasket and put that in the trunk with her. Then he drove around all night.

He called his sister and told her what had happened. She urged him to call the police. He did that the next morning. The officers met him at Fifth and Main Streets, where he waited outside his car. He told them his wife was in the trunk of the car, and he was waiting for her to knock to be let out.

When the trunk was opened, Marcia's body was there, wrapped in the bedspread. The wastebasket with her had Inn at the Quay printed on it. Patterson was hustled off to jail.

Detectives went to room 160. Housekeeping staff had been there, and the room had been made up. The bloody sheets were in the laundry room across the hall. The bloody pillow had been discarded, and the bedspread was reported stolen. Two bullet wounds would have made a horrific mess. There was no mention of that.

Patterson was arraigned, went to trial and claimed it was an accident. He just liked to shoot holes in things, he explained, cacti, for instance. He dearly loved to shoot holes in the Mobilgas Flying Red Horse signs. Mostly, he liked to shoot pillows. They'd argued, he admitted, but he just wanted to shoot holes in the pillows. The gun just went off, accidentally, twice.

The jury believed him, and they found that the state had not proven that it was murder. He walked away. If I were Marcia Elaine, I would haunt that hotel room. I would haunt the courtroom, too, and the judge and all twelve jurors.

Jackie Charles Patterson went back to Arizona, where, a month later, he was arrested for trying to run down a man with whom he'd argued. From Arizona, he moved to Oklahoma, where he met and married another woman. Soon after, she disappeared. He said they'd argued, and she'd left him. Then he met another woman, a stripper. He shot her in the leg. She escaped, and he was arrested again.

In July 1990, the police found Jackie's second wife, Cynthia, buried under a concrete slab. She'd been shot just as Marcia had been. When the police caught up with him this time, Patterson shot himself in the head. After all, he just liked to shoot holes in things.

WEBBER MACHINE

A short walk up Columbia Street is a tan brick building that, at first glance, seems very modern. But then you notice the darker intricate brick design and realize that it's older than it looks.

It would seem that spirits do not always stay in their era. Maybe they can take advantage of modern times. One such spirit is a shade that appeared reflected in a computer screen. Workers in the former Webber Machine Works have reported the shape of a man moving behind them, reflected in the computer screen. He moved slowly, painfully. This happened when they thought that they were alone in the building.

The sad story did not take long to find. Webber Machine was a beloved business in Vancouver. Kids could take broken parts of their bikes to be repaired or duplicated. Inside, it was a marvelous sight. There weren't separate electric connections for each of the machines, so great belts whirred from machine to machine, across the ceiling and down.

Joseph Webber, the founding owner, had begun his working life in Vancouver as a blacksmith. His shop was at his house at that corner. He and his sons worked at the Standifer Shipyards during World War I.

When the war ended, he started a blacksmith shop at Fourth and Columbia and built a home there. He and his wife had sons, Harry and James. He grew his blacksmith business into a machine shop. Eventually, his sons came into the business with him. He built a finer house. In 1921, they built the handsome structure you see today.

The Webber family operated their machine business near Fourth and Columbia Streets since before World War I. *Author's collection.*

Joseph aged, and his wife died, He mourned her passing. Soon, he lived alone with a housekeeper and her daughter. Life and the company were passing him by.

He found himself to be forgetful, slowing and confused. Early on February 3, 1946, he arrived at the shop. The day after Groundhog Day was clear—the temperature in the forties. His son Harry was already at the house. They greeted each other casually. Nothing was out of the ordinary.

He sat down at a bolt bender machine. With a carpenter's pencil, he wrote out a short note: "I'm getting to be a burden, Goodbye." With that he shot himself in the heart.

The business continued for many years. Occasionally, someone would be brushed. A clerk at a desk felt a hand on her shoulder, just briefly. It would be cold around the bolt bender.

The machine works closed eventually because there was no longer a need for small machine works. The building was converted to office space. Other businesses moved in. Computers came with the new businesses. Each desk soon had a computer. Later, employees saw the reflection of an old man who wasn't there.

Evergreen Hotel

At the foot of Main Street, at Fifth, is the Evergreen Hotel. It opened with a grand gala on March 17, 1928. Evergreen—green for St Patrick's Day. It had a meaning.

Narrow Fifth Street was once the main route east and west. It was the only road that crossed the military installation. Since Washington Street was the main road north and south at that time, the route that connected to the Interstate Bridge, the location was perfect for a hotel. Unfortunately, no one could be found to build it. The chamber of commerce formed a corporation, sold shares and raised enough to build the inn.

Built in the grand Spanish style, it boasted a nightclub called Alexander's. Some of the biggest acts in show business played Alexander's. Today, the hotel is an assisted living facility. Alexander's is no more. The dance floor is carpeted. That's why it's decidedly odd to occasionally hear the sound of tap-dancing feet. Perhaps this is a case of a tap dancer coming to a bad end there. Perhaps it's a return to a former triumph. Perhaps it's bad plumbing.

In the depths of the Great Depression, the City of Vancouver sold shares in the Evergreen Hotel to raise the funds to build it. *Author's collection.*

There was a tap dancer murdered during the hotel's heyday. I cannot tie him to the Evergreen Hotel, although he performed there often.

The Ray Vance case was an unsolved murder. His face looks out of the newspaper's front page, top hatted and with a boutonniere in his lapel. He was a popular vaudeville entertainer in 1931, born and raised in Vancouver. He grew up in the Hough Neighborhood near the courthouse. He traveled around the West Coast dancing and was seemingly successful. He was happy and well liked. He had not a care in the world and was happily married—not an enemy to be found.

Vance had been set on his career by none other than Vancouver's long-serving mayor John P. Kiggins, who had taught him his first tricky tap dance steps at the old USA Theater in Vancouver.

On February 24, 1931, Vance disappeared. A Portland policeman, Charles Lamb, and his wife dropped Vance off at the gates of Lotus Isle, an amusement park of the day. Lamb said that Vance would walk the rest of the way.

Months later, on June 13, Vance's headless body was found floating in Lake River at the Columbia. His wife, Violet, identified him from the rosary he carried, a handkerchief embroidered with his initial and bits of paper scribbled with jokes for his act. The Clark County prosecutor, Dale

McMullen, said that it was obviously a murder and must have happened in Multnomah County. Dr. W.E. Cass, the coroner concurred, referring to the lack of a head.

Lotus Langley, the Multnomah County prosecutor, along with the Multnomah County chief deputy sheriff, were equally adamant that it was a suicide and must have happened in Clark County, possibly by jumping off the Interstate Bridge.

Yielding to pressure, Prosecutor McMullen sent a hearse to pick up the body. Dr. Cass refused to release it. Then both coroners and both prosecutors dropped out of the case. Both referred the case to the other.

The story of Vance began to change. He did have marital problems, he did have enemies, people did owe him money and what about that Portland policeman? The episode came to an end with both jurisdictions criticizing each other. No charges were ever filed, no one was ever arrested and no investigation was ever made. Ray Vance was quietly laid to rest in St. James Cemetery.

He had performed often at the Evergreen, but at the time that he died, he was headed to a job in Seattle. Could he be the dancer in the hotel? It would be a stretch to connect him, but that's the closest that we've come.

FIRST NATIONAL BANK

Connected to the Evergreen Hotel building is the small jewel of a building covered in terra-cotta tiles. It is a studio for glass artists today but was originally the home of the First National Bank. Over the years, people working in the bank, and other workers as the building's use changed, complained of being touched. People said they felt someone close behind them, watching what they did. Again, and again, the feeling of being watched was brought up. One man said that he'd gone looking for the person spying on him.

Charles Brown was the president of the bank early in the twentieth century. E.L. Canby was the cashier. Both were from leading families. Canby was married to Frances Burnside, and both families were Oregon pioneers. Brown was the son of Samuel Brown, the first receiver of public monies, appointed by President Lincoln. He was married to Rebecca Slocum, another old Vancouver family. They were sterling members of society.

One morning, Brown and Canby were faced with the unthinkable. The State Bank examiner was at the door. There was a suspicion that questionable

The First National Bank was built of molded stone in 1910.The terra-cotta facing was added in 1926. *Author's collection.*

loans had been made, accounts had been embezzled and money had been transferred from account to account to hide the losses.

As the bank examiner worked, Canby became more and more nervous, until he finally blurted out the truth of the embezzlement. He grabbed a revolver and ran out the back door of the bank. He pulled the trigger, but the weapon failed to go off. Half hysterical, he came back into the bank and grasped Charles Brown's hand. "We are caught," he said.

The examiner took the pistol, but Brown took another gun from a drawer, and the pair left the building. They stopped near a playground where Canby's son often played and stood for a few minutes. Canby's son was not there. They continued on to the corner of Twelfth and Columbia Streets and peeked in the windows of Brown's home.

Then the two began to walk north, past the Columbia School on Kauffman and then another mile north to a field that would one day become Thirty-Ninth and Kauffman. Canby scribbled a hurried note in pencil to his wife, urging her to live for their children. Then he shot himself. Brown took the gun from him and repeated the act. He fell forward over his friend's body.

I asked one of the glass blowers in today's studio if he ever had the feeling of being watched. He snorted, "Ma'am, that's why I'm here!"

Charles Brown House

The tragedy of Charles Brown spins off into yet another reportedly haunted dwelling. Charles Brown and his wife, Rebecca, lived in a charming French Second Empire house that had been built in 1866. It's one of the oldest houses in Vancouver and is now used as law offices.

Those working in the offices have heard people moving about in rooms that proved to be empty. Upstairs windows rattle, and lights are turned on or off.

Charles Brown did stop at the house on his way to his tragic end. He and his wife had been married in that house, and their children had been born in it. He had celebrated his election as city councilman there and then four elections as county auditor. It must have torn at his heart to peer in the windows of the home where he had known such joy and triumph and to know that he left it in shame and humiliation.

Heritage Building

Diagonally across the intersection of Sixth and Main Streets stands the Heritage Building, once called the Ford Building and before that the First National Bank.

The Brown house still stands on West Eleventh. Built in 1883, it's one of the last Victorian-era homes in Vancouver. *Author's collection.*

The United States National Bank, now known as the Heritage Building, was built in 1012 in the Chicago Modern style. *Author's collection.*

A private investigator who had offices in the building, Dean Cavilee, related a tale about an after-hours resident. He also told this story to his son. Dean was surprised one evening to see someone on the stairs late in the evening. He was dressed in rough work clothes, and when he saw Dean, he disappeared. "As if you'd thrown a light switch," Dean said.

In those clothes, he was obviously not a professional man in the building. There had once been a man in rough working clothes who tried to hold up that bank. As he lay dying, repenting all that he had done, he said that he had cased the bank from the mezzanine and thought he had planned the perfect crime.

Joyce Thomasen was an unlikely criminal, the son of a well-respected Oregon farmer. He worked in Portland for a horse dealer. He had come to town to accompany his mother to a convention of pioneer families. He had, however, already pulled one robbery with a friend from high school. Now he lurked on the mezzanine and watched the bank. The next day, prepared, he returned.

On that day, as the employees arrived, he shepherded them into a back room. One teller, Joseph Langsdorf, saw something amiss. Thomasen wanted the safe open. Langsdorf told him the safe wouldn't open and then bolted. When Langsdorf escaped, Thomasen decided to run as well. Alerted by Langsdorf's shouts, police rushed to the scene. Thomasen ran into a house, and Harry Williams, the sole Washington highway patrolman assigned to Clark County, followed him and shot several times through the bathroom door. Thomasen fell, hit by several rounds. It took a few days for him to die—long enough to regret his crime.

Could the man in rough clothing be Joyce Thomasen? Is he still pondering the mistakes that brought him down? Or is he plotting how he could have done it better?

Parking Building

On Seventh Street at Broadway is a building that has been converted to a parking garage. It's a squat, square concrete-block building with a front covered in plywood. There is a paved area next to it. It's not an attractive building, and not one to notice.

One evening, a man was going to his car, and he saw something odd. On the Broadway side was a man wearing a white shirt. He was fiddling around with something. Was he a prowler or a car thief? He called out. The man faded away.

Was that building always a garage? No, of course not. It had, for a time, been a thrift store, and before that it was a Safeway Market.

On a Saturday night in April 1945, the forty-eight-year-old store manager, Clarence Sebo, was locking up to go home. Markets in that day had an open front with doors that pulled across the opening. Usually two or three people would work together to lock up, but this night Sebo was alone. Out of the dark, three men appeared. They struck Sebo over the head and shot him. The bullet pierced his left side and lodged in his abdomen.

The side door is in the same place that it was in 1945. Is Mr. Sebo still trying to lock up and go home as he did that Saturday night so long ago?

A Parking Space

There is another parking structure downtown with a horrific story. This tale was just told recently. The building is a set of walls—no roof or windows and a curved front. It seems to be waiting for completion or destruction.

A patron of the building volunteered his opinion that the structure is haunted. He had seen nothing, but he had feelings of sudden terror as he approached his car—not panic but sheer terror. There was no reason to fear, he told himself, he was a healthy middle-aged man. The terror is accompanied by the overwhelming need to escape. He is shaking by the time he gets to his car. He said that he is glad that he has a fob because he would not be able to get a key in the lock. At last, he gets inside the car and behind the wheel. His breathing is shallow and gasping. As he reaches the street, the feeling eases. It's not every night, fortunately, or he'd be compelled to look elsewhere for convenient parking. But it happens often enough that it concerned him. The story he heard gave him reason to believe that he is not losing his mind but tuning into a past tragedy.

It was a full-moon night on November 8, 1995. Veterans Day was just ahead. The Bonsells, father and son, Walter II and Walter III, called Morry, were in the auto body shop. Morry's dog, Fast, was there too. The father was working late. He wanted to get ahead of schedule so that he and the boy could go hunting together. They planned to leave Thursday after school. Walter and Fast would pick Morry up at Hough School, and they would head off.

Once a car dealership and then an auto repair shop, this structure has been a parking site since the devastating fire. *Author's collection.*

Wednesday night, Morry tied Fast to a bench and laid down on a cot at the back of the shop. A stray spark ignited one of the volatile liquids. Within seconds, the shop was an inferno—dull thuds and small explosions marked its progress. Walter made it outside with burns over 27 percent of his body. Passersby restrained him as he tried to get back into the shop for his son.

Flames leaped up the wall of the neighboring Heritage Building. The Vancouver Fire Department attacked the blaze from the street and aimed the hose from the roof of the Heritage Building. Morry's mother was called, and she raced from Portland to the scene. Walter sat on the curb, weeping and calling for his son.

"If Fast is not in the building, my son made it out," she cried. Very soon, they found the remains of Fast, still tied to the bench. Morry was found under the collapsed roof in the rubble. The boy, anticipating a hunting trip with his Dad and his dog, awakened to the roar of an inferno and the roof collapsing around his cot. The terror lingers.

KIGGINS THEATER

The Kiggins Theater was designed by architect Day Hillborne for Mayor John P. Kiggins in 1936. It stands as an example of Art-Deco/Moderne design and reflects the elegance of going to the movies, which was the style in the 1930s and '40s.

In most towns, the old single-screen movie houses have closed, converted to other uses or razed. The Kiggins Theater has been rescued and restored. Movies old and new, as well as live programs of community interest, guarantee few dark nights in the old house.

The owner, Dan Wyatt, has said that on going into the projection booth, he will sometimes see a shadow pass quickly across the little room. No one can pass in or out of that small space without being seen, of course, and no one ever is.

There was a couple sitting in the front after the movie was over. When an employee went to tell them that the show was over, there was no one there. There have also been glimpses of a woman on the stairs who is not there a second later.

These are incomplete stories. There is no justification to be found. There have been no tragedies here and no sorrow. The Kiggins suffered a devastating fire in 1944, but that was late at night, causing no injuries. During the time that the building was closed and empty, passersby could catch a faint whiff of popcorn. There was no one there to pop the corn.

One of Mayor John P. Kiggins's theaters, the Kiggins was built in Art Nouveau style by architect Day Hillborn in 1936. *Photo by Dana Beasley.*

At one time, a movie date was the norm. Often, it was a first date and sometimes the last. Maybe a soul is waiting for someone who isn't going to be there. Or maybe it's just someone returning to a place of happy memories.

Next to the theater is a wine bar called the Niche. Leah Jackson, the owner, affirms that her place was not haunted. It had been a children's shop in its prime. Next to the wine bar, Leah has an art gallery. That is also free of haunts, but the basement has a quirk.

Everybody who goes to the basement forgets why they're making the trip. Leah said, "It's like there's a memory vacuum that sucks the thought right out of you."

HIDDEN HOUSE

On Thirteenth Street downtown is the Hidden House. In fact, there are two of them, both made of brick. One is on the corner of Main Street and one is on Washington Street. They aren't really hidden, of course, you can see them plain as day. They were built by the Hidden family. For generations, they were in business in Vancouver, making bricks and investing in land and businesses. Once, their brickyard was at Fifteenth and Main Streets. From these houses, it was just a short stroll to work.

When the family moved on, the house was home to Clark College. Later, it became a restaurant. One unseen guest seems to enjoy just staying in the

The Hidden House as the Blueberry Inn in the 1960s. The two brick buildings in this block of East Thirteenth Street were both homes to Hiddens. *Author's collection.*

house. She sings and greets employees as they arrive sometimes. She doesn't like things left overnight on one particular table, so she knocks them onto the floor during the night. Some personnel didn't like to be too early for work or to be the first one there. Others grew fond of her.

Try as one might, there is no tragedy or scandal to be found in that house, nor any theatrics that would cause a spirit to sing.

There was, however, a member of the family who was noted for her lovely voice: Julia Hidden, who married John Wesley Todd. She did sing frequently. She was one of the few young women of her era who went away to college. She sang at church, for her mother's women's club and for her Eastern Star chapter. A respectable young woman could not go on the stage, mercy me, but she could sing for society, and that's what Julia did. Perhaps she still does.

CLARK COUNTY HISTORICAL MUSEUM

Another unexplained spirit seems to stay in the Clark County Historical Museum at Sixteenth and Main Streets. There had been gossip about the building, but then one day, things changed.

The first inkling was when one of the curators, Doug Magedanz, a pragmatic young man, stayed late to do some refurbishing of one of the rooms. As he was a diligent worker, it was a surprise to find the work unfinished the next morning. The paint roller was left in the pan. He had left abruptly. All he would say about what happened was that "something didn't want me here."

There was, at one time, a railroad section in the basement of the museum. There were railroad artifacts and a large model train set that depicted the Spokane, Portland and Seattle line (SP&S) through the Columbia Gorge. There was a large gray desk by the entrance, behind which a volunteer from the retired ranks would sit. One afternoon, a volunteer came upstairs to ask, "Who's playing tricks on me?" No one had been. She said that as she sat at the desk, she heard a child's voice, softly crying, "Help me. Help me."

Everybody trooped downstairs and investigated. Nothing was found. Several weeks later, yet another volunteer heard the same thing. The director, working after hours, heard a rapping. He went into the office. "Did you knock?" he asked staff. No one had knocked. Several times, the staff has checked the heating system, people outside the building and traffic noises, all to no avail.

The Carnegie Library, now the Clark County Historical Museum, opened on New Year's Eve in 1909. It looked like this in the late 1930s. The large tree at the rear of the building is a cutting from the Witness Tree. The small tree in the front is the elm that would grow to cover the entrance. The ivy would be removed. *Author's collection.*

One day, a volunteer in the research library glanced up and looked right into the eyes of a young boy. The boy then disappeared. The volunteer also left quickly.

The building was built as a Carnegie Library. It opened on New Year's Eve 1909 as a wonder. It was the first public building in the city to have electric lighting. The opening was held in the evening to show the lighting to its fullest. It did, of course, have gas lighting as well, as they mustn't put too much faith in radical new concepts.

It served as the city's library until 1963. A new library was built then, and the building became the museum. The railroad exhibit was located in what was once the children's section of the library. Nothing has ever happened in the building that would account for a child in distress. Indeed, all of the people who return to the building now who once used it as children have nothing but happy memories of the place. The train exhibit was eventually replaced with a workspace.

The only mystery that I have been able to uncover is a bricked-up door under the stairs. It would open under the surface of the lawn, so it could not have been a door outside. Was it a closet? Libraries and museums would never sacrifice a closet. When a new concrete porch was built in 2018, a void was discovered under the steps, but no investigation was made. Sadly, the door is now hidden behind a shelf.

The only unpleasantness that happened in the building was early on. It was not a tragedy, except to the members of the Grand Army of the Republic (GAR). The GAR, an organization of Civil War veterans, was evicted from its meeting room downstairs due to lack of space. The resulting furor resulted in resignations, name-calling and letters to the editor and a right royal dustup in the city. Peace was finally restored, of course, and the problem of the GAR was self-canceling due to age and mortality. I would look to one of those old veterans to be hanging out down there or maybe one of the early librarians, but neither would match a plaintive child's voice calling, "Help me. Help me."

Chumasero House

The Chumasero House is in the National Register of Historic Places. It was a bed-and-breakfast for several years and is now offices. It wasn't always where it is not. It was moved from Harney Street after the death of Alfred Chumasero. Alfred was the town's pharmacist and was in the group that started the town's water company. With his brother-in-law, he began the first electric company in town.

It has been reported that doors in the house will swing shut, and if closed slowly, they will swing open. Lights downstairs have suddenly come on by themselves. One night, the owners were startled by a rapping at the window. That could have been explained away, but the tapping came from inside the room.

What do we know about Alfred Chumasero? He was the area's first settler of Filipino descent. He moved here in 1893 from his birthplace in Iowa. His father had come from the Philippines to the United States via New Orleans. Alfred was born in 1861. His father enlisted in the Union army during the Civil War and lost his life in the conflict. Alfred was then raised by an uncle and given a fine education at Oberlin College.

When he arrived in Vancouver, he opened his pharmacy at the corner of Sixth and Main Streets. He married a local girl, Mary Estelle Smith and, with her brothers, invested in other successful businesses.

Soon after his arrival, the agitation with Spain began, which led to the Spanish-American War. As his business prospered, he saw the troops from Vancouver Barracks, under the leadership of General Thomas Anderson, head to the Philippines. Then began the Aguinaldo Rebellion against the

Alfred Chumasero in his pharmacy on Main at Sixth Street. He died on February 23, 1923. *Author's collection.*

Americans. How difficult it must have been for Chumasero to watch his birth country and the country of his heritage locked in a struggle. The Aguinaldo Rebellion ended in 1902, the year that the house was built.

As troops marched past his drugstore toward yet another war in 1917, Alfred fell ill. As a pharmacist, he knew that there were no drugs to save him from tuberculosis. In his home, he slowly wasted away, until his death in 1923. The city changed the name of his street to Chumasero Street. Today, after the streets were alphabetized, it's named Harney.

The presence in the house is described as a gentle being, which fits. Alfred loved the grand old house when he lived in it. I am sure he would love the care and attention that the present owners have given it. Maybe he just feels at home.

DuBois House

Residents in the DuBois house on Esther spoke of a ghost at their residence. This one never makes it to their door. Footsteps on the porch, a gentle knocking at the door and one would expect a caller. There is never anyone there. There are no sounds or apparitions inside the house—only on the front porch.

Two young boys lived there with their grandmother and their mother. One afternoon, Edward and George Burton went off for a jaunt on their bikes. It was late in April 1918. The wind blew a frosty thirty-seven degrees. It was much too cold for spring. They were bundled up in scarves, gloves, hats, sweaters and jackets. Only young boys would rather be on their bikes than huddling indoors. The United States had been at war for not quite three weeks. Already, soldiers were marching at the barracks, and the sound of hammers rang from the Standifer Shipyard. Excitement filled the air—so much for boys to see and wonder at. By nine o'clock at night at Vancouver Junction, they had reached the railroad tracks. There was a train stopped there, idling. They pushed their bikes around the back of the halted train. They did not see that there was another train coming. With all of the cold weather gear, perhaps they did not hear the sound. Edward, the oldest boy, was struck and killed. The younger, George, survived. But he was horribly traumatized.

The shaken train crew carried the child's body to Ridgefield. A funeral home picked up the shattered remains. He was brought back to Grandma's house, where he was laid out in his little coffin in the parlor until the funeral at St. James Church two days later.

Is the ghost on the front porch that little boy, Edward, still trying to get home to Grandma's house?

Slocum House

An old house stands, rather peculiarly, in Esther Short Park. It has been a theater and a winery. In its incarnations, especially as a theater, strange happenings have been reported. A young woman has been seen wafting up the stairs. When the house was a theater, she would pull costumes off their hangers.

I've found no evidence of wrongdoing in the house or in the park. There is a tale that Esther Short's husband, Amos, shot and killed emissaries from

The Slocum House at its original location on Esther Street, not long before it was moved to Esther Short Park. *Author's collection.*

the Hudson's Bay Company in the park area. It is true that he committed that killing, but it was not at that location

The house was moved two blocks to Esther Short Park in 1966. Robert Hidden, a prominent citizen, with the historical society, managed to save this one old building in an early Vancouver neighborhood from the hungry jaws that were urban renewal—a blight that swept the country during the 1960s.

The house is unique. It is the only house in Vancouver with a widow's walk around the roof. Charles Slocum was a successful businessman in early Vancouver. He was a supplier to the army and operated several general stores in the Northwest. He assisted in laying out the town plat of Boise, Idaho. The house is thought to reflect the homes of his boyhood in New England.

There were no problems for him in that house. He didn't even die in the house. Before his death, he built another house closer to the railroad depot on Jefferson Street. In 1909, the elite believed that would be the new center of town. The railroad had crossed the river at last, and surely, everything would move closer to transportation. The large houses that the town built near the tracks soon became boardinghouses or were divided into apartments.

The young girl is a mystery, then. Perhaps she is a servant girl or a relative who still hangs around.

FIRST PRESBYTERIAN CHURCH

At Evergreen and Daniels is a brick church building that was once the home of the Columbia Arts Center. It was originally the home of the First Presbyterian Church. It was completely remodeled when it was an arts center. Now it is a church again. It has a caretaker that works twenty-four hours a day, it would appear, but very few can see him.

In the theater years, an actress discovered a man standing by the wall of a dressing room one evening. She gasped, and he faded away. She saw him clearly—a tall man with a beard, dressed in dark clothing. She did not see it as black garb, but dark. A volunteer found the same man standing near the furnace in the basement. He also disappeared when she challenged him.

Arden Williams attended the church as a young man. He said that the spirit in the church was often seen. It was usually just a shadow outside a door, but sometimes it had the shape of a man.

He said, "Once, I was sitting in the choir loft, when I heard the floor creaking along the passageway. Well, of course it is an old building, and floors creak, but this was footsteps."

The First Presbyterian Church was built in 1885. It served until 1957, when the current church was built on Main Street. *Author's collection.*

"I kept reading my book," he continued. "And those footsteps came into the choir loft, came right up and paused behind me. Needless to say, I fled."

Had anything happened in the church? No, not in the church itself, but something awful had happened.

The year 1929 was a bad one for Clark County. Horrendous fires had roared through the forests, threatening homes, villages and towns. It had been a long, hot summer, indeed. Sunday, September 29, was another hot day. After church that day, Reverend Charles Baskerville, who'd been pastor for ten years, decided to have a picnic with his family. Joined by Dr. Dwight Parish and his family, they drove to the Columbia River. About a mile below Blurock's landing, they set up their dinner on the shore. Barbara Baskerville, his fourteen-year-old daughter, decided to cool off with a wade in the water. Her mother joined her. They laughed and splashed each other lightly. Suddenly, the mother disappeared. She had stepped into a hole. Dr. Parish saw her sink and leaped in to rescue her. As he rushed into the water, Barbara vanished too. Parish saw Reverend Baskerville jump into the water. He assumed that Baskerville would swim for the daughter, who was closest, as he rescued his wife. He brought his wife ashore and saw no trace of the pastor. He leapt into the water again and brought in his daughter. The Reverend Baskerville was nowhere to be seen.

They called for help as Dr. Parish tried to calm the distraught family. Reverend Baskerville's body was not recovered until a makeshift dragline was put into the river. By then he'd been underwater for two hours. A pleasant late summer outing had rapidly turned into tragedy.

Almost everyone in town turned out for the funeral. Charles Baskerville had been active in almost every organization in the city. His three brothers, also Presbyterian ministers, arrived to mourn. His congregation was distraught. Letters of grief poured into the local newspaper. That Sunday morning, all had been normal; Sunday night, everything was hanged.

Maybe Reverend Charles Baskerville is the sad-looking man in the church. He truly was devoted to the church and its people. The building has been scheduled for demolition. Will the sad caretaker of the building finally find rest then?

Courthouse

The courthouse was designed by noted architect Day Hillborn in the Art Deco/Art Moderne style. The county dedicated it on November 29, 1941.

That was a Saturday, and the country would know just one more week of peace. The building has obviously held its share of drama since then.

The top floor of the county courthouse held the jail before the newer sheriff's office and jail was constructed in 1985. The cell that held the most dangerous prisoners is now the storage room for janitorial supplies. Today, the janitorial services in the county courthouse are performed by crews from Innovative Services. Some of the employees were unnerved by a shape—not quite a shadow but also not solid—that seemed to follow them as they worked on the top floor of the building.

Once, the elevator rose and the doors opened, although no one had called it, there was no one in it and the building was closed. One young man, who will be called Everett, said that he was shaking so much that he could hardly hold onto his tools. He said it was the fastest that his team had ever finished that floor.

In November 1954, husky, blond Phillip Lyons was waiting for his trial for two assaults. He'd beaten his wife and her sister. He was a navy veteran of World War II with a Purple Heart. He had married a fetching nursing student just three years before. Yet here he was—his life apparently ruined, and this future unsure. Lyons wrote a note to his wife and then began to

The Clark County Courthouse was a Day Hillborn's design. It is in the Art Deco/Moderne style and opened in 1941. The jail was on the top floor. *Author's collection.*

methodically rip his mattress into strips. Patiently, he braided the strips and then made a noose. He threw the improvised rope over the jail bars. He was found the next morning, hanged in his cell.

Is Phillip Lyons one of the regretful souls who roam the floor of the former jail? Is he the shadow that follows the workers? It seems a shame that the shadow will never know release.

STEAKHOUSE

Two waitresses from the Black Angus Steakhouse downtown came into the museum one afternoon, trying to find out what caused the problems in their place. They described a feeling of not being alone at closing. They'd put out all of the candles on the tables and find that the ones in the back were lit again. The room had partitions, and they were sure that someone was behind the partitions watching them. There were thumps and bumps at the back of the room when no one was there. One said that she would have the male bartender walk her to her car at closing.

Where the restaurant stands today was once the site of St. Joseph's Hospital. Before the state took over the care of the mentally ill, the Sisters of Providence tended those patients.

Mother Joseph, born Esther Pariseau in Quebec, came to Vancouver with her little band of nuns in December 1856. She looked around the town and immediately saw what the town needed most. She opened the Sisters of Providence Lunatic Asylum. The sisters cared for the mentally ill until the state took over their care. They expanded the asylum to a general hospital, St. Joseph's. That little one-room hospital grew into the Southwest Washington Medical Center with two campuses. It's now Peace-Health Hospital. They tore down the old St. Joseph's Hospital, and the restaurant was built there.

The two waitresses went away satisfied—they had the answer to their ghost but still didn't want to be there after closing.

MOTHER JOSEPH

We must digress here to tell a little more about Mother Joseph. An incredible woman with multiple talents, she built hospitals, schools and orphanages.

Mother Joseph of the Sacred Heart led a group of nuns to the Pacific Northwest in 1856. She died in Vancouver in 1902. *Author's collection.*

She cared for the dying, the aged and the destitute. She had no money, of course, as she had taken vows of poverty, chastity and obedience. The obedience part gave her a little trouble. We know that she often wrote to the bishop apologizing for being bossy or cranky or hard to get along with. To get the money she needed for her works, she begged. She went to the gold fields, for, as Willie Sutton had said, that's where the money was. There she would make her plea for donations for the work she was doing across the Northwest. With her was usually a young and pretty nun. She reasoned that no one would give money to a homely old woman, but they'd shell out handsomely to a pretty and innocent young girl. It worked like a charm. The money came in, and the building went up.

As the first woman architect in the Pacific Northwest, she designed and built the Providence Academy that still stands on Evergreen Boulevard. Local legend has it that it was she who convinced Mr. Hidden to make his first bricks so that she'd have building materials. She was a carpenter, a wood carver and a sculptor of wax statues. She carved in plaster, embroidered, gardened and sewed. She is credited with designing, if not actually carving, the pews at St. James Church.

There is a story that during the great flood of 1893, the Columbia River rose inexorably toward the hospital and academy. Mother Joseph placed a statue of St. Joseph at the edge of the garden. "Protect our hospital, dedicated to your name," she prayed. The river's rise stopped at the feet of the statue.

Mother Joseph died in 1902. Her grave, at St. James Acres on Fourth Plain, is a National Historic Site. Her statue stands in front of Vancouver City Hall, in the rotunda of the Capitol in Washington, D.C, and in the state Capitol in Olympia.

Her lasting monument here is the academy, which has its own stories to tell.

PROVIDENCE ACADEMY

When the academy was built in 1873, it was the largest brick building north of San Francisco. Over the years, it served the children of Vancouver not only as a school but also as an orphanage.

In 1969, it was going to be demolished. A developer envisioned the Academy Condominiums. Robert Hidden, the twentieth-century patriarch of the old family that had made the bricks from which the building was built, saved it. He bought it and converted the interior into office space and a wedding chapel and rented out the old auditorium for receptions and parties. It was a convenient spot for many professional people, in the heart of downtown.

One of the tenants would spy a little girl darting around the corner toward the stairs. She made no sound, though. And try as he might, the tenant could never catch up with her.

Another tenant, a well-respected CPA in Vancouver, had his offices there once. He worked late one night and was alone in the great old building. He had to let himself into the building and knew that there was no one else there. He'd left the door to his office open. He heard a definite sound of footsteps coming down the hall. Since he knew he was alone, he was concerned. The steps passed his office. No one was there. He jumped up from his desk and ran to the door. No one was in the hall. His offices are now in another building.

An architect rented an office on the second floor. As he was working late one night, he heard footsteps on the third floor. He was nervous, as he was there all alone. Investigating, he found that there were no doors unlocked that led into the third floor. There was no one there. He realized, while exploring the area, that this section of the building had contained the living quarters of the nuns who had taught at the academy. He heard the footsteps above his head often after that, but he paid them no mind. He just hoped that the nun who wandered the room would say a prayer for him once in a while.

Everyone who gets to go up into the attic wants to ring the bell and then put their initials on the rail around it. A volunteer working in the attic felt profound sadness whenever he went near the bell. He said that it was "like a miasma" as soon as he came within touching distance of the bell.

There is a tragic story around the bell. When the academy was closed as a school in 1966, the nuns had the bell removed and taken to Issaquah to be stored. In 1975, when Robert Hidden bought the building, he asked that the bell be returned.

Above: Providence Academy as it looked in 1937. It was dedicated in September 1873. It was designed by Mother Joseph and built with Hidden Company Bricks. *Author's collection.*

Right: Some visitors can ring the academy bell. If they do, their initials are inscribed on the windowsill of the tower. *Author's collection.*

The 104th Division at Vancouver Barracks had two Huey helicopters assigned. Two men volunteered to fly to Issaquah and bring the bell home. Army reserve captain Arnold Kraushaar and a civilian employee, William Kinney, were the men who would make the trip. Four miles after takeoff from Toledo-Winlock Airport, the Huey crashed into a stand of trees near the freeway. Fragments of the helicopter were scattered along the trail left by the Huey to where it lay in a small crater. Neither of the men survived.

Could the sadness experienced by our volunteer be a result of the loss of two men sent to bring the bell home?

2
Officer's Row and the Barracks

Going into Vancouver's Historic Reserve is entering the most haunted area of Clark County. There have been more reported sightings there than anywhere else. This green 680-acre swath in the center of the city was once the military reserve. It originally swept from Fourth Plain Road to the shore of the Columbia River. It stretched from West Reserve Road, now under the freeway, to East Reserve Road. The U.S. Army arrived here in 1849 and located on the rise above the Hudson's Bay Company. The troops used some Hudson's Bay houses but needed more housing for officers. The soldiers were put to work building nine log homes. The homes were not what you would call luxurious. Officers called them "corrals with roofs on them." The wind blew through them, and the chinking fell out in the winter. All in all, they were miserable places to live. The best of them was a sturdy two-story log house built for the commanding officer. It still stands; we call it the Grant House. Through the years, the other log hovels were, one by one, replaced with the gracious and stately homes we now call Officer's Row.

Grant House

The house in the center of the row is the Grant House and is now a popular restaurant. It was the first commanding officer's residence. That would have

The Department of the Columbia, formed in 1865, covered Washington, Oregon, Idaho and California. After 1871, it also included Alaska. It was absorbed into the War Department in 1891. *Author's collection.*

The Grant House was built of logs in 1849. It was the commanding officer's home. The weatherboarding, window and door casings were added in 1856. *Author's collection.*

been Brevet Major John S. Hatheway. Ulysses S Grant, for whom it is named, never lived in the house. He shared quarters with the other quartermasters. Colonel Benjamin Bonneville lived in the house when Grant was stationed at the barracks.

When newer residences were built for commanding officers, the house became a library, then bachelor officers' quarters and then an officer's club. There have been reports of hauntings for years. When it was an officer's club, some soldiers would joke that there was another guest for cocktails that afternoon.

After World War II, the house was declared surplus by the army, and it became a bridge club and then a museum, operated by the local Soroptimist club. The curator, David Freece, had a tiny apartment on the second level. He and his wife, Janet, lived there with the museum cat, Chadwick.

The front door would open and close, and steps could be heard upstairs when no one was there. The orange museum cat followed something around the house. Whatever it was, Chadwick was intensely interested in it.

One afternoon a woman appeared at the door of the Grant House, proclaiming herself a sensitive. She introduced herself as Laura, saying she had heard of the ghost in the house. She wandered through the house, pausing here and there, until she reached the upstairs east front bedroom. Chadwick followed her, staying well back.

"There's a military man here," she said. Well, that was a good guess, since it was officer's housing. "A tall, thin man, with dark hair, very melancholy."

That did describe General Alfred Sully, who had died in that room in 1879. A melancholier man you cannot imagine. He had good reason to be too. After graduation, Sully served in the Mexican-American War. Later he was posted to California. There he met Manuela, the beautiful teenage daughter of a Spanish grandee. They fell in love and married. Manuela's papa gave the young couple a gristmill and some ranch land. Life was good. He wrote ecstatic letters home to his sister of the wonderful life he was living.

Soon, Manuela gave birth to a baby boy. A former suitor sent a basket of fruit to the young mother. Alfred wrote to his sister that he had not trusted the man and had warned Manuela not to eat any of it. She laughed and took an orange. She soon fell ill, fainting and moaning in pain. She was taken to bed, and a priest was sent for. Sully watched in anguish as she suffered through the night and died.

Manuela's mother, who was probably in her thirties, took the baby into bed with her to wet nurse. In the night, she rolled over on the infant, suffocating him. Sully was never the same. Never would he have the joy of life and optimism he'd had before. Eventually, he would remarry, but the memory of Manuela was always there. Certainly, Manuela would always be young and beautiful.

He served through the Civil War and the Indian wars. He was cold and brutal then and frequently came under fire for his tactics. He grew world-wearier. When his posting came to Vancouver Barracks, he felt it was in the nature of a punishment. With his family, he journeyed west. He was already ill with what was called chronic indigestion, the condition that would ultimately kill him. His health slowly deteriorated.

He went off with General Howard in the pursuit of Chief Joseph but was too weak to ride a horse. General Custer referred to him as "the general who goes to war in an ambulance."

Sully served at the barracks as he weakened. Unable to be as active physically as he had been, he began once more to paint. He painted the Grant House, Government Dock and Mount Hood. Most of his paintings survive, owned by his family and the United States Military Academy at West Point.

Good news came to Sully in 1879. His old comrade in arms U.S. Grant was coming back to Vancouver for a visit. He began making preparations for the former president, but his evil star struck for the last time. He died a painful death on August 27, 1879, missing his old friend by three months.

Perhaps the sorrows and regrets of his life were just too much, and he still roams the old house. Perhaps it's just an ancient log house settling, moving and creaking.

Another psychic, accompanied by the AM Northwest's television news team, toured the house early one morning. Everything went wrong. The person with the keys failed to show up, there was a power failure at the television station, there was an accident that knocked out the phone lines, the crew's cellphone batteries died. The psychic said, "There's someone here, and he's laughing at us now."

Once inside, at the top of the stairs, she exclaimed, "He's right here." She described a man who liked to be important and felt important there in the house. In the west room upstairs was a group photograph of the family and staff. She pointed to a figure. "That's the man at the top of the stairs," she said. She put her finger on the image of Alfred Sully.

A former owner of the restaurant, Suzy Taylor, described seeing a man cross at the top of the stairs. She asked her staff who was upstairs. When she was told that there was no one there, she was delighted—she had actually seen the ghost.

A MODERN-DAY TRAGEDY

A more modern relict is in a two-story double duplex near the Grant House. Here a tenant complained that there was a stain on the floor of the upstairs bedroom. No matter how hard it was scrubbed, it wouldn't come out. The stain bothered him. He didn't want to look at it. He put a throw rug over it but still felt it was there. In this room, a cold draft would blow through occasionally, even though no doors or windows were open.

Friends and family said that Sonia Petersen was a strong-willed young woman. Things were going to be done her way, there was no question. Her mother admitted, "You never know what she's going to say."

Sonia had declined college, although she'd been an outstanding student. She married, against the advice of everyone. That soon ended in divorce. She wanted a baby, which she accomplished as well. The child brought some stability. She went to secretarial school and found a job. She moved in with a friend, Michelle Nagle, in a quaint century-old duplex on Officer's Row. Michelle had the bedroom in the front of the house, Sonia was in the back and the little one slept in a room next to hers.

Several of the Officer's Row houses are available for private home rentals. One of the duplexes was the scene of a tragic crime. *Author's collection.*

Sonia met an attractive man, Jeffrey Kern. He had a great smile and curly brown hair. He also had a criminal record for burglary and receiving stolen property. He was on parole. That romance was short-lived too. In April 1987, there was a prowler outside the duplex. Sonia called the police. She told them it might be Jeffrey, but the police log says the prowler was gone by the officers' arrival.

The row had been busy, and there were people coming and going. There was an exhibit opening at the Marshall House, the fiftieth anniversary of the Valery Chkalov Transpolar Flight. Soviet bigwigs and Chkalov's son were expected. There were diplomatic snafus and political games to be played. All of this was to culminate on April 10. That was probably what had alarmed Michelle and Sonia. Sonia and Michelle went to bed.

No one knows for sure what happened the next morning. Sonia was getting ready for work. She had her makeup on, her iron was on and a skirt was ready to be ironed.

There was a struggle, and Sonia ended up dead in a pool of blood on the floor. Michelle knocked on her door when Sonia missed her morning coffee. She found Sonia's body and called the police. She told them about Jeffrey, and Sunday morning he was taken into custody.

Life went on for Sonia's family and Michelle Nagle. But the spot on the floor won't go away.

GRIEVING INDIAN WOMAN

A stroll down Officer's Row is a stroll through history and an avenue of ghosts. At the western end of the row, by the freeway, is a troubled spot. It seems to be just a parking area now, bordered by the concrete and foliage barrier of the freeway. There have been sightings of an elderly Native American woman who simply sits, head bowed, and then fades away. She appeared to be wrapped in a cape, blanket or shawl. If it was a reed cape, it would place her in an early era. A blanket from Hudson's Bay would be later, and an army blanket would be after 1849.

Before the Hudson's Bay Company arrived, the Chinook placed their dead in canoes and lifted them onto high places. The Hudson's Bay Company started a cemetery to the north of the fort. With the Great Sicknesses of the 1840s, the Chinook abandoned their practice of open-air funerals and began burying their dead at that cemetery.

Most of the restored houses on the row are used as professional office space. Some have extra, unseen staff. *Author's collection.*

The army arrived in 1849 and also used the cemetery. The town sprang up, and the townspeople used it. Eventually, the army built a new cemetery just north of where Evergreen now crosses the freeway. As before, townspeople used it. In 1867, it was closed to civilian burials. Then, in 1881, civilians were asked to relocate their loved ones. There were seventy-two disinterments in that year. That must have been a banner year for gravediggers.

In 1883, the Post Cemetery of today was built at the uppermost northwest corner of the Military Reservation. Today that is on Fourth Plain Road at the Interstate 5 Freeway.

Local legend has it that not all of the graves were moved. And that appears more likely than not. On at least one occasion, a coffin was found under one of the existing buildings. Maybe that's why the old woman sat there. Maybe she was distressed over the loss of her grave. Maybe she mourns a loved one who was there—or maybe still is.

One afternoon, some workers in the house on the end saw an odd tableau. There had been a small archaeological dig at the end of the road. There are often archaeologic explorations across the Historic Reserve. This time they saw that the archaeologists had been joined by a Chinook shaman who was praying. That is not as common. Perhaps that ceremony let the woman rest. She has not been seen for a long time.

It did not, however, lay all reports to rest, at least not in that house. The westernmost house on the row was occupied by a technical company that worked in energy and dealt with utilities and engineers across the West. This is definitely not a workforce given to flights of fancy.

One of the staff was Traci Meyer-Jones. One day she heard someone walking upstairs. No one should have been there. She went upstairs and turned the knob on the door of the upstairs office. Suddenly, the door was jerked out of her hand and pulled wide open. No one was there. Traci hastily retreated downstairs to collect herself. No one came downstairs, and no one left the building. The room upstairs stood empty—no one was there.

The engineers, realists all, heard someone pacing upstairs. What could have caused that? We pace when trying to make a decision. We pace when we are worried, angry or impatient. The pacing seems to have continued.

The same group of engineers performed a truly engineer-like experiment to verify another haunting. People in the house would catch whiffs of cigar smoke. Smoking was, and is, not allowed in the house. Yet frequently a wayward scent of tobacco would drift by. The engineers devised an experiment. They stationed themselves at regular spaces on the stairway. The instruction was to raise your hand when the aroma of tobacco was caught. One by one, from the top of the stairs to the ground floor, each of them raised their hand.

"It was never a frightening experience," Traci Meyer-Jones said. "We just lived with those people we couldn't see."

O.O. Howard House

The O.O. Howard House, which stands just south of the traffic circle at Evergreen and Fort Vancouver Way, has had an illustrious history and has a few ghosts of its own.

The first occupant of the house was General Oliver Otis Howard, a man of contradictions. He was a valiant soldier who always carried a bible. He'd risen through the ranks during the Civil War from colonel to brigadier in just a few months. At the battle of Fair Oaks, he lost an arm but returned to the battlefield in just five months. He was praised and equally humiliated for decisions that he made. He received the Congressional Medal of Honor for valor. At the end of the Civil War, he was placed in charge of the Freedman's Bureau to determine how the nation should handle the thousands on thousands of freed slaves. He had grand programs but no administrative ability, so the bureau was infamously corrupt. He founded Howard University, which grew into one of the finest Black universities in the nation.

He led the pursuit of Chief Joseph of the Nez Perce across the Northwest, almost into Canada. Joseph's courage and military tactical ability won the respect of the soldiers who pursued him. Howard eventually settled surrender terms with him.

After Howard moved on, General Thomas Anderson lived in the house. He was the longest-serving commander of the barracks. Anderson was also a Civil War veteran and had been wounded in that war. He led the Washington Volunteers to the Philippines during the Spanish-American War, which was the first expedition of American troops in Asia. At the end of the war, he and troops from Vancouver Barracks fought in the insurrection that followed.

He was a short man who had a voice that could be heard across the parade grounds. His troops called him the "little orator." He loved to act and started a community theater group and acted in the plays they produced. After his death, the Scottish Rite Masons held a torchlit midnight parade and ceremony in his honor.

The Marshall House replaced the Howard House as the commander's dwelling, just as it had replaced the Grant House. Other officers occupied the house through the years. Later, it became an NCO Club and served in that use until a fire almost destroyed it. After the fire, it was boarded up.

There have been some strange goings on in that house. Figures have been seen moving through it, and people say that you don't want to go into the basement. Even as pragmatic a person as Lieutenant Colonel Royce Pollard, then base commander and later mayor of Vancouver, saw a figure inside the house.

Colonel Pollard's house was across the parking area from the Howard House. Walking across that area one day with his son, he saw a woman in a second-story window. The house was boarded up; no one was supposed to be there. After an investigation, it was determined that no one was there. In fact, he found, there was no floor in front of the window on which anyone could stand.

The City of Vancouver took possession of the house and restored it. It became the offices for the Historic Trust and for the third district congresswoman. Restoration didn't clear out all of the inhabitants, though. The burglar alarm went off. The alarm showed a progression—first the ground floor, then the stairs and then the second floor. Then the exhibits began to shatter.

Each area was set off with a five-foot sheet of heavy glass, exquisitely etched from actual photographs of the era. The etchings represented real people and places. The first one shattered while being installed. The second while the house was locked up for the night. Obviously, it was a defective piece of glass. Then the third one exploded. The last panel has been remounted with rubber cushioning to keep it from breaking. We'll see.

What might have caused all of this? If hauntings are caused by tragedy or high emotion, you need look no further than a military base—the separations, the despair or the fear. The death notices in the military columns in the local newspaper had more than their share of suicides, accidental deaths and sorrow.

MARSHALL HOUSE

The grandest house on the row is the George C. Marshall House. A five-star general during World War II, Marshall went on to become secretary of state under Harry S. Truman and crafted the Marshall plan for the recovery of a Europe devastated by war. He is the only career military man to ever receive the Nobel Peace Prize. But before all of that, Marshall lived in this house on Officer's Row.

Marshall and his wife were happy here. They wrote fondly of their stay in this idyllic location. Only the war called them away. There are noises in the house—great thumping in the basement and footsteps overhead. Who could it be?

The grounds of the houses were maintained by military prisoners, soldiers sentenced for minor offenses. Katherine Marshall grew quite fond of some.

Long before the Marshalls, at the end of the nineteenth century, there was one who had been sentenced for being drunk, not an uncommon offense. He was different. John M. Walden had been a well-known, up-and-coming lawyer in Chicago. He journeyed to Seattle on a business trip. While there, he got drunk and enlisted in the army—not as an officer but as an enlisted man.

There seems to have been no way out of that. In September 1898, far away from Chicago and in trouble for drinking again, he hanged himself

George C. Marshall served in Vancouver before becoming chief of staff in 1939. He is the only military man to receive the Nobel Peace Prize. *Author's collection.*

in the back of the house. His body was not returned to Chicago, and he is buried at the Post Cemetery. Perhaps those thumps and bangs are from a man full of regret for the shambles he'd made of a promising life.

The Lady in White

On the northwest side of the traffic circle, on the corner of Fort Vancouver Way, is a grand house dominating the corner like a dowager queen. There are offices there now, but it was once a home. Army officers and their families lived there in comfortable style. As did most families then, they had servants.

One of the servants still lives in the house. She has been seen on the stairs. Phones light up when there is no one there to use them. Lights go on and off. Sounds are heard coming from the attic. Once a pale woman in white was seen on a stair. Could it be the lovely Nan?

She worked for a young officer and his family as a nanny. A secret romance developed, and the inevitable happened. Nan became pregnant.

The graceful trees along Officer's Row were planted by prisoners at the direction of Nelson Miles. Replacement trees are planted by schoolchildren. *Author's collection.*

The officer disavowed her, denied responsibility and refused to help her. She was ordered to leave the house. It can be believed that the officer's wife was more than anxious for her to leave.

Nan was in despair. She knew what lay ahead. Life was not easy for an unwed mother in the nineteenth century, nor was it easy for a child of such a union. Nan knew that she faced shame and contempt and so did the child. It became too much to bear. One last time, she climbed the stairs to her attic room and hanged herself. She is seen occasionally, still dressed in her white cotton dress, on the stairs and in her room. She is one of the ghosts on the row who seems drawn to babies. Since she was a nanny, she had a natural inclination that way.

Another ghost who loves babies is said to dwell in the small house that is the second east from the traffic circle. She seems to be a sweet spirit. Babies who fret or cry while living there have an unseen hand that rocks them gently. A rocking chair that was in the house gently rocked by itself, as though a ghostly baby needed comforting too.

A stroll through the Post Cemetery on Fourth Plain reveals many small headstones of children. Scarlet fever, diphtheria, whooping cough and measles carried off many little ones in those days. Sometimes you see that several died in the same outbreak in the same family. Could they be the origin of the many stories along this row of houses?

Farther east on the row, in one of the duplexes that have been converted to townhouses, the occupant has decided that she simply has a roommate that she cannot see. Doors open by themselves in that unit—upstairs when the tenant is downstairs and vice versa. The ghost, who the resident feels is an older woman, is also appreciative of the rocking chair in the living room. She rocks in it quite regularly.

GHOSTLY DRUMMER

A resident near the east end of the row swears that he has heard tattoos played on a drum far away but very clear. He only hears it late at night, and he has asked his neighbors if they have heard the rat-a-tat. None had. There was a time when signals were sent on the battlefield by drum. Every outfit had a drummer boy who was too young to be a soldier but old enough to march into battle with his drum.

In October 1872, one such boy got drunk. There was a lot of drinking on the post in those days and no age limits. The drummer boy was thrown into the guardhouse to sober up. Somehow, an argument broke out between the drunken boy and his guard. The guard shot and killed him. The sheriff demanded the culprit, but the army refused. After much angry debate, the

The guardhouse at Vancouver Barracks in the Spanish-American War era. *Author's collection.*

To get the mules' ears to stand at attention, the man who regularly fed them would beat on a bucket behind the photographer. *Author's collection.*

army kept the prisoner for court-martial. Just as well, too, or there might have been the ghost of a lynching to deal with.

Late at night, listen for the faraway sound of a drum. Remember those brave young lads who marched with the men into battle, beating out the signals on their drums.

Still on duty? Maybe mules have ghosts too. Early one morning, a runner was surprised to see a team of mules on Fifth Street. He thought that there must be a reenactment coming up, so he changed his route to take a look. He was surprised when he rounded the corner, and there were no mules. There was not even a trace that mules had ever been there. Believe me, mules would have left traces.

The runner came into the museum, still in his running clothes. He swore that he saw mules—a mob of mules. As he was an airline pilot, however, he didn't want to give his name.

Many years ago, there were indeed mules there. The army ran on mules. The redbrick building that stands on the corner of McLoughlin and Fifth Streets was the mule barn. It has been lovingly restored and is used as office space by the Washington Department of Transportation. Maybe they didn't clear out all of the old occupants.

The Auditorium

The army auditorium is a building that looks like a chapel but is not. It is on McLoughlin Road in the barracks. That building has attracted more than its share of attention. There were sounds of people walking about, but, as usual, when one would go to investigate, there would be no one there. The soldiers called it "coexistence." They worked during the day, and the ghosts worked at night. Since one did not bother the other, life went on at the post.

The auditorium was built on the site of the old cemetery that had been used by St. James Church when it stood on Fifth Street across from the fort. The church had claimed the land around it under the Missionary Law, which granted churches 640 acres. The army also claimed the land. It would seem that even 150 years ago everyone wanted a piece of the action in Clark County.

The army and the Catholic Church would eventually square off against each other in court, and the army would win. St. James built its new church in town at the corner of Thirteenth and Washington.

Before the auditorium was built, the graves had been moved. Some, unmarked, were inadvertently left behind. In 1982, while digging for a water

There was a pistol range in the basement of the auditorium for many years. The directive to clean up the lead contamination led to strange occurrences. *Author's collection.*

pipe in the basement, workers were taken aback when they found human remains. There was a coffin and a skeleton that had been buried without a coffin. Nothing was done about this for more than a decade. But the building was no longer quiet. Doors slammed with no one to slam them. Often, after an event, chairs were carefully stacked, only to be found pushed across the room the next morning.

When Colonel Ward Jones was assigned as barracks commander, he had an order to clean up the basement—not for the graves but for lead. The basement had been used as a shooting range during World War II and the Korean Conflict, and there were thousands of rounds of lead left. That can make the air unhealthy, unless you are a ghost already. When he heard the whole story of the graves and the skeleton, Jones called Roy Wilson, a holy man for the Chinook and Cowlitz tribes.

Wilson told the colonel that the spirits were unhappy and restless since the disruption of the graves. A cleansing ceremony was performed in the basement. He burned sage and, in the smoke, used an eagle feather as he prayed for the cleansing. He returned the next day to make sure that all of the spirits were appeased. So far, there have been no new reports in that building. Then again, perhaps the spirits are still on the night shift.

When Jones was first assigned, he was working alone in the headquarters building. Above him, he heard voices and the sound of footsteps walking about. He assumed it was the medical unit preparing to leave for a training assignment. When he finished work, he went upstairs to tell them that he was off for the night and for them to secure the building. No one was there. That was curious.

The next night, the same thing occurred: he heard the sounds of people moving about, voices and chairs scraping on the floor. Again, there was no one there. The next day, he asked some of his men if they had ever heard things in the building. They looked at each other and said, "Shall we tell him?"

Yes, they should. They told him that it was just the ghosts in the barracks that he heard and that they minded their own business and the soldiers minded theirs, and they didn't bother each other.

Jones told the *Columbian* newspaper that shortly after his arrival, as he walked past the main hall in building 638, which housed his offices, he saw a woman with light brown hair walk from his office to his secretary's. She was wearing an old-fashioned dress that reached the floor, and there was a scent of lilacs wafting through the air. Curious, he followed her into the room. His secretary, who had dark hair, was at her computer terminal alone. She had seen no one, and she had been alone in there all day. The scent of lilacs

The headquarters of the 104th Infantry Timberwolves was closed by the Pentagon. That unit moved to a location on the east side of Vancouver. *Author's collection.*

remained. Maybe the woman was the wife of a soldier or a sweetheart. She still remains in the building, they say, drifting through.

A sergeant, who on occasion stayed in the barracks overnight, was awakened by a call to attention. There was the sound of boots.

Rushing up the stairs, he found that no one was there. He was alone, and it was two o'clock in the morning. Convinced that he had a most peculiar and vivid dream, he returned to sleep. A couple of nights later, though, he was again awakened, this time by a pool game in progress upstairs. Once again, he hurried up the stairs, and once again, the room was deserted. This time, the balls on the pool table were still in motion.

The large barracks building on McClelland Road was home to the Washington National Guard and the army reserve until they moved on to their own headquarters in 2010. One evening a soldier in a World War I–era uniform appeared. The figure approached a soldier doing some late work.

"What are you doing in my building?" asked the shade.

The soldier snapped back, "You get out of my building!"

The First World War soldier did just that, vanishing like the lid of a box had snapped shut. The soldier said out loud, "What the hell just happened?"

A sand table of Camp Bonneville was set up in that same building. One morning the company clerk opened the room. The terrain on the sand table had been altered. That would have been enough, one would think, but in addition, all of the pictures on the wall had been flipped over, and file drawers were open. The clerk could hear the sound of snickering in the corner of the room. He left.

POST HOSPITAL

The large brick and white wood building that you can see from the freeway in the reserve was once the barracks hospital. You do get an eerie feeling in that building, if only because you remember the primitive medicine that was practiced there.

They had little in the way of anesthetics, ether mostly, and they used natural light, hence the many windows. The operating theater was in the area with many windows to take advantage of the light. In that area, the windows are sometimes broken out from the inside. There is no one there. It could be intruders committing malicious mischief, but there have also been scratches that appeared on the outside of the windows. This is on the third floor, mind you. There is a connection to the basement.

Lieutenant Doug Luse, of the Vancouver Police Department, searched in the building late one night. It was cold and dark. In the basement, he came across a door leading into a small room. It had a thick glass window with bars on it. He knew what a holding cell looked like. The cell could have been used to contain a mentally ill patient or, more frequently, a violently drunk one. He went back to search for that room sometime later, but the doors had all been changed.

The morgue was in that basement of the hospital too. Undoubtedly, autopsies were carried out in that area. More disquieting, there are pipes leading from the upper floors. The hospital was built just before electric lighting came to Vancouver, so operations, amputations and other procedures were carried out in the upper floors in the rooms with large windows. The floors were tile and had drains in the center. When operations were concluded, the blood and fluids would be washed down through the pipes to the basement. This was state of the art for the day.

There is a rude ghost hanging around in the building. An employee received a hard shove one day. She turned around, and no one was there. After she had been rudely jostled a couple more times, she left. As would anyone.

The hospital was built with open porches for outdoor sleeping. The rainy climate of Vancouver quickly led them to enclose the porches. *Author's collection.*

A clerk was approached by a young GI. He was wearing an out-of-date uniform. "I'm looking for my buddy," he said. "I'm looking for my buddy." He turned from the speechless clerk, walked down the hall and vanished.

Elsewhere in the building was the gangrene ward. Before asepsis, and before antibiotics, gangrene was an ever-present danger. Modern-day troops working in that area have complained of cold, aching limbs, as well as an acrid stench. Would the memory of that awful condition still linger in these rooms?

A young Native American woman, Victoria Mortek, lived in one of the brick homes in the barracks near the hospital. Her husband was stationed at the barracks, and she worked there too. They lived there until they retired and then settled in Armada in Vancouver. She served as president of the local YWCA. Later she told me that she would never walk toward the hospital. When she went to work, she would always head in the opposite direction from the building. She said it was always too crowded around the hospital. She could sense crowds of spirits wandering around the grounds.

There is a specter that can almost be felt on the barracks grounds, and that is the flu of 1918. Today people are again comprehending the terror of that time. The pandemic had ravaged the soldiers in Europe, but the news of the sickness had originally come from Spain, hence the nickname Spanish flu. It caused destruction around the world and came to Vancouver in October 1918. The army and the city health officer had seen it coming.

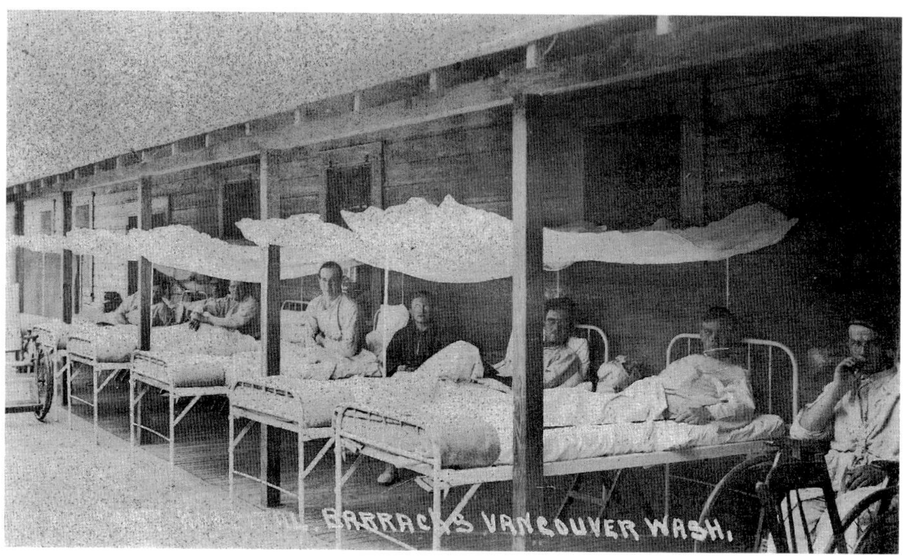

Soldiers recuperating at Vancouver Barracks in about 1910. *Author's collection.*

It had hit Seattle and caused two thousand deaths. Together they urged the city government to shut down the city—everything must close except restaurants. The city council heeded their words and closed everything down one day too late.

The barracks were crowded with soldiers. To add to the congestion, there were thousands of civilian and military assigned to the Spruce Production Division turning out spruce for airplanes. The spruce mill occupied the land where the Pearson Airfield stands, as well as where the Hudson's Bay fort has been rebuilt.

A soldier's wife had brought the flu from Oklahoma. The next day, there were six patients. In the next few weeks, six hundred would die on the barracks. It is unclear exactly how many died in Clark County because the recordkeepers died as well. Some called it the "three-day flu." In three days, you were either recovering, they said, or you were dead. Sometimes it killed quicker than that. Victims drowned in their own fluids, pink froth coming from the nose and mouth.

The armistice was declared on November 11, the Spruce Production Division ceased operation on November 12 and General Disque began selling the components of the mill the next day. There were those then who declared they felt the spirits of the dead workers wandering through the gigantic buildings of the mill.

There are mutterings and murmurings heard throughout the hospital building. They're not quite distinct enough to distinguish word or sentences but are definitely human voices. One was clearer than the others.

Annette Emerson, a county resident, related the story as told by her husband, an electrician who had worked in the hospital. "Just mutterings," he'd told her. "In a foreign language but not Spanish or any Latin language." He thought it was a European language, maybe German. When the German prisoners of war were in Vancouver, however, the hospital was no longer in use.

Many immigrants joined the army to attain American citizenship in the early days, so it was not unusual to find citizens of many countries serving in the military. Sometimes things did not go well for them. This was true of poor Corporal Anthony Breiter. Breiter was a native of Bavaria and had been in the army for twenty years. He was a man of good reputation and was married with two children. He served as the company barber.

One early morning in 1906, Breiter returned to Vancouver after a weekend leave spent in Portland. He was wearing civilian clothes. He joined several other soldiers in Weigel's Saloon on Main Street, where they were drinking beer before returning to the Barracks for reveille.

In the bar was Private Thomas Anderson, no relation to General Anderson or his son, Colonel Thomas Anderson. Private Anderson was from Sweden and was the company cook. He was reputed to be a heavy drinker. His comrades said that while they rarely saw him drunk, at no time in the past four years had he been completely sober.

Just a few hours before Breiter entered the saloon, Anderson bought a pistol and some ammunition. When Breiter arrived, he was challenged by Anderson. Anderson told him to step outside. Other soldiers told him not to go, but Breiter insisted, saying that he'd rather solve any problem right away. Shortly, two pistol shots were heard, and they ran outside to find Breiter on the ground. They overcame Anderson and held him down until police arrived.

They transported both Breiter and Anderson to the Post Hospital. Breiter died soon after from his wounds, and Anderson was treated for the injuries he sustained at the hands of his fellow soldiers. Perhaps what Mr. Emerson heard was Corporal Breiter as his life ebbed away or Private Anderson muttering in Swedish as he awaited his transfer to the guardhouse.

PEARSON FIELD

Pearson Field was named for Alexander Pearson, a young daredevil army pilot who was killed practicing for a speed run. Could he be the lone figure sometimes seen walking out of the airstrip? Probably not, as he was not killed at Pearson.

A horrible event was rediscovered after a civilian pilot, making an approach to Pearson, thought he saw a wrecked plane on the field. He looked again and saw an empty field. He was not about to mention it to anyone, as he was concerned for his pilot's license. After a few weeks, he came into the museum, researching plane crashes and found the story he wanted all by himself.

On a cool June afternoon, Lieutenant Henry Goode came to Pearson Field. He was a reserve pilot and had brought along his wife, Elizabeth, to watch him fly. Goode was from an old Portland family. His father had been the president of the Lewis and Clark Centennial Exposition in Portland, and he had graduated from Yale before joining the army. He had been an officer in the infantry but had resigned his commission to go into aviation. He'd just been commissioned as a lieutenant the week before and was a pursuit pilot.

There was a crowd there, among them young Lieutenant Julius Syfford. He was not a pilot but wanted to fly. The group watched Lieutenant Oakley Kelley fly his big de Haviland. At around four o'clock in the afternoon,

Alfred Chumasero in his pharmacy on Main at Sixth Street. He died on February 23, 1923, at the age of sixty-one. *Author's collection.*

Kelley landed and handed the plane to Goode. Goode and Syfford climbed into the plane and took off. It had only gained about two hundred feet of altitude when the crowd noticed flames shooting from the right exhaust line. The de Haviland had thrown a rod.

Goode banked to turn back. Kelley was shouting, "Shoot for the river, shoot for the river!" One wing tip hit the ground, and the plane crashed in a ball of flame. Syfford was thrown thirty feet and was terribly burned. Goode was thrown out, but the plane rolled onto him, pinning him under an engine. He burned to death. Syfford was taken to the base hospital and survived.

Our pilot was satisfied. He had not, he felt, been wrong. He had indeed seen a crash on Pearson Field, but he was just a little more than seventy years too late.

The Fort

Fort Vancouver is a reconstruction of the Hudson's Bay Company trading fort that was operating from 1824 until 1860. That old British company is the reason that the city exists today. Situated on the great river, near the confluences of other rivers, it was ideally located for trade with the Chinooks and other neighboring tribes. American immigrants could trade at the fort for goods that they needed to start their new lives. The company urged them to go south into American territories in Oregon. The territory north of the Columbia River was British, they maintained.

In 1846, Britain and the United States signed the treaty that drew the international boundary at the Forty-Ninth Parallel. In 1849, the army arrived, and by 1860, the company had moved to British Columbia.

There have been few tales from the fort. One, in fact, would seem to have no connection to the Hudson's Bay Company at all. A teenage girl, Finch Tiffaney, with her mother, visited the fort. As they approached the gates, she noticed a man in an 1860s-era army uniform.

"He wasn't transparent, or misty. He was solid, just like anyone else," she insisted. "But he gave me a hard stare as we approached and as we passed by him. I tapped my mother on her arm to call attention to him, but he was gone, just like that!" The fort often has reenactments of Hudson's Bay life, and elsewhere in the Historic Reserve, there are costumed interpreters. The volunteer at the gate, however, told her that there were no programs scheduled that day. When the fort did reenactments, she added, it would be of the Hudson's Bay, not the army.

The Hudson's Bay Company built a fur trading fort on the Columbia in 1824. Beaver pelts were needed to make hats. They intended to "trap out" the area. *Author's collection.*

She is adamant that what she saw that day was a ghost. The spirit of a soldier of that time. During the Civil War, The Barracks was manned by the Oregon Volunteers, what we would call today the National Guard, so a shade from that time would not have been too far from home.

BARNES HOSPITAL

There's hardly anything left of the old Barnes Army Hospital, but it was once a sprawling complex of wooden structure built to serve the casualties of World War II. It was named for Dr. Joseph K. Barnes, surgeon general from 1862 until 1886. He had the dubious honor of being at the deathbed of President Abraham Lincoln and then later at the side of James Garfield.

It is now a modern facility of veteran's services, as well as the county health department. It hugs the northwestern corner of what was once the Military Reserve along Fourth Plain. Most hospitals seem to collect ghosts, and this one is no exception.

One report stands out. It was related by an ultimate pragmatist, Victoria Ransom, a member of the museum board and a former Women's Army Corps officer. Her story began one night when an orderly heard a voice outside the building. No one should have been out there, and no one was. The voices had sounded agitated and were unintelligible, perhaps foreign. The voices faded away.

Sometime later, he heard them again. He knew that there was supposed to be no one outside. The voices would sound far away and then close. He was sure that there were two voices. He advised security that he'd heard the voices more clearly, and they were not speaking English. Security found nothing; no one was there.

Who could these men have been? An almost forgotten story from World War II may have the answer. There was a prisoner of war camp in the barracks. It was not a secret—anyone driving west on Fifth Street would have driven right past it. The earliest prisoners were Italian. When the United States entered the war in Europe, there were thousands of prisoners, and there was no room for them. Almost 500,000 Axis prisoners were sent to the United States. They were assigned to camps across the United States. Vancouver took about two hundred Italian POWs at first.

They were originally housed at Pearson Field, until a cantonment could be built for them farther north, about where Hudson's Bay High School is today. The prisoners were issued uniforms that were identical to our army's uniforms, but with no insignias. Occasionally, a few of them would escape on a weekend and head for the USO, where they could dance with girls until the military police came to round them up. As punishment, they'd be sent to Camp Bonneville, where they did stonework. Vancouver Barracks was probably one of the few POW camps that had relatives of the prisoners come to visit. It was just an overnight train trip from San Francisco.

Barnes Hospital received its first patients, casualties of the Aleutian battles, on April 26, 1945. Later that year, actress Rita Hayworth visited the patients. *Author's collection.*

Midway through the war, in 1943, Italy surrendered and came in on the Allied side. What to do with the POWs? Technically, they weren't prisoners of war anymore. They were, however, still in the Italian army and still had to obey their own officers. We couldn't send them home because there was a war going on.

They became noncombatant aliens, or cobelligerents. Some found jobs on farms or at Kaiser Shipyards. We gave dances for them. Some found girlfriends, a development that caused no end of resentment when our young men came back from the war. When the war ended, they were rounded up and returned home, but not all of them made it back.

At Christmastime in 1945, the war was over. We were trying to get everything back to normal. Italian army sergeant Vincenzo Dioguardi decided to go to Portland in an army Jeep to do some shopping. Private First Class Peter Sinisgali, an army interpreter, was driving. They were having trouble with the Jeep's headlights; they'd dim and brighten.

At about 6:15 p.m., south of the bridge, they dimmed again. As they brightened, a truck loomed up in front of them. Sinisgali swerved, but the passenger side of the Jeep hit the truck. Sinisgali was unhurt, but Dioguardi was severely injured

The truck driver said he'd call an ambulance but then left. An unidentified soldier came to the jeep and decided to drive Dioguardi to the barracks hospital. He died on the way. Could he be the angry voice outside the hospital? So near to going home and yet so far?

Or could it be one of the other POWs, German and Italian, who lie buried at the Post Cemetery? There is Jakob Planke, Frederick Leonhardt, Burbien Biambick and Apostolic Beneduto, or perhaps the young Russian soldier, Elisbar Elisbaraschwili, who died here and lies near them.

Each Memorial Day and Veteran's Day, when the town decorates the graves at the cemetery with American flags, there will be Italian, German and Russian flags fluttering over the resting places of those young men who died so far from home so long ago. Soldiers resting with soldiers.

3
KAISER SHIPYARDS

On the banks of the Columbia River today stands a modern industrial park. Giant trucks scurry through like roaring juggernauts, and the hurly-burly of modern manufacturing echoes across the river. It is easy to imagine what the place would have been like in the 1940s. You can still see the enormous buildings that stand there—great gaping halls of steel along the river that were the Kaiser Shipyards.

The Pacific Fleet was decimated at Pearl Harbor in 1941, and the Pacific Ocean stood open for the enemy to control. In February 1942, just two months later, the Kaiser Company announced the plan to help rebuild the fleet.

The Kaiser Corporation and the Permanente Cement Company had been engaged in building dams up the Columbia River before the war. Managers had noticed Ryan Point jutting out into the river. The Hidden family had a farm there on a distinctive triangular point of land. It was a perfect site to build and launch the great ships that would be needed. By July, less than five months later, the yards were open, and the ships were already taking shape. The quiet little town of Vancouver would, in that same period, go from eight thousand people to a population of over eighty-five thousand.

That yard would turn out 141 ships. One ship was built, from laying its keel to floating in the river, in seventy-one and a half hours. It would have been impossible to continue at that pace, with thousands of people working, without injury or death. The safety standards of the day were enforced, but the odds were against them. And death and injury happened.

Kaiser Shipyard was begun in February 1942. It was completed and launched its first ship in April. It operated twenty-four hours a day. *Author's collection.*

LOST IN THE RIVER

The first of our haunts was actually reported from the Oregon side of the river. A couple had gone exploring near the Portland Airport on Marine Drive. They climbed the high levee there. As they looked toward the Washington side, they saw a strange-looking boat making its way across the river. When they looked directly at it, it was gone.

Eventually, the couple came to the museum. As they described the boat, it sounded rather like a tug, yet very much like a ferry. But our ferryboat had run from the foot of Washington Street before the Interstate Bridge was built. The ferry had been out of business since 1917. We began to search. The following is the story we found.

The streets of Vancouver and Portland, Oregon, became crowded with cars. Traffic often came to a standstill. The bridge was overcrowded, carrying too many cars back and forth between the Swan Island yards and the Vancouver yards. To add to the traffic woes, the lift span of the bridge had to be raised frequently for the ships that were being built and the cargo ships making their way up the river to the yard and to factories beyond.

To ease the congestion, trucks were hooked up to trailers fitted with wooden benches, and these served as buses between the housing projects and the factories. A tugboat was pressed into service to push or pull a barge outfitted as a passenger craft between the shipyards and the airport across the river.

The winter of 1942–43 was cold. By January 22, sixteen inches of snow had fallen. Two days later, another two inches fell. The temperature was so low that people claimed the mercury in their thermometers had frozen since it did not move. Many of the shipyard workers had migrated from warm southern states. They weren't used to Pacific Northwest weather. Passenger numbers had dropped dramatically because of the weather. Although they would later deny it, the tugboat operators decided to leave the barge tied up and just run the passengers across on the tug.

In the early hours of February 11, nineteen men boarded the tug for the trip across the river. It must have been particularly raw on the water. They were dressed for the cold in sweaters, coats and gloves. The frigid water was choppy, and the wind was bitter and piercing. As many as could fit were crowded inside, away from the biting wind.

The tug foundered and sank. Those inside quickly perished. Some who jumped into the icy water were weighted down by their heavy clothes and were lost. Ten of the nineteen souls aboard the tug were lost. The silence of the disaster made the horror worse.

Could that have been what the young couple saw that early morning: the tugboat ferry and the men still trying to get to the Kaiser Shipyard? Those are not the only spirits wandering Ryan's Point.

HUDSON HOUSE

Another problem caused by the shipyard and the population boom was where to put all the new people. The Vancouver Housing Authority built thousands of homes, and for the single men and women, two sets of dormitories were erected. Columbia House was built north of the railroad tracks, and Hudson House was built to the south of them. The Vancouver Housing Authority estimated that the dormitories had housed ten thousand workers over the

Onlookers marveled that anyone escaped the inferno at the Hudson House in November 1942. *Author's collection.*

years. Portco, a packaging firm, took over the theater for the Hudson House as the area was converted to an industrial park.

An employee of one of the buildings to the south of that Portco structure complained of a strange discomfort in her building. She experienced a lassitude, along with a sense of sorrow—a feeling of grief with no cause. Nothing in her life would cause such emotion. Then she learned that a few other employees felt the same malaise. They discussed it over coffee and came to the conclusion that something must have happened there. Indeed, it had.

Late at night on November 13, 1942, a fire erupted in dormitory D. The security guard blew his whistle to wake everyone but had to flee the explosive onrush of the flames. With a roar like a blast furnace, the fire raced through the flimsily built two-story structure. Later it was speculated that the flames had reached the furnace blower, and that had blown the fire throughout the structure.

People leaped from windows or jumped through flames to escape. Those who made it out later said that they didn't remember fleeing. One man who fled left his prosthetic leg behind and never figured out how he had done it.

Soldiers guard the scene of a fatal troop train crash in the shipyards on March 24, 1942. There are echoes of the disaster still heard. *Author's collection.*

Herbert Carson, the yard's chef safety inspector rushed to the scene. He said, "I don't see how it can be possible that they all got out. I feel sure that there must be several in there."

He was right. When it was over, seven people were dead, and forty people were injured. Florine DuFresne, wife of a funeral director, helped the coroner try to identify the bodies. Some, she later said, could only be identified by the contents of their stomachs. "You could tell by the contents what shift they were on by what they'd had for lunch." Four of the bodies were never identified. The personnel records were destroyed with the building.

Two years later, in 1944, there was yet another deadly fire in the Hudson House dormitory, with two lives lost. Such events could cause an impression of sorrow and loss. The shipyards were converted to an industrial park. Trucks and trains rumble in and out. Hundreds of people work in the area.

Phantom Train

Late one night a security guard was startled by the unmistakable shriek of a train braking at speed. It sounded as though it was right in front of him. It had been a quiet night, and he had thought it would be a good time to break for coffee. Then came the metallic scream. If you're a security guard in a truck all alone late at night and you hear that sound that close, you will definitely want to know where it is in relation to your body. He certainly did.

He drove to all of the grade and spur crossings around the industrial park and found no trains. His hands were shaking as he drank his coffee. Several weeks later, he heard the same sound. Again, he looked for anything in the industrial park that would make that noise. He found nothing.

He visited the museum, asking to look at maps and aerial photos of the area. He was looking for a railroad spur that he had missed but found nothing. He was most embarrassed to tell his story. He did not want to admit that such an event could happen to him.

Maybe what he heard was the echo of an old disaster. Late in the night on May 22, 1942, as crews were working day and night to construct the shipyards, an SP&S passenger train carrying troops en route to Vancouver Barracks was almost at its destination.

Three men were in the locomotive's cab: fifty-four-year-old engineer Walter Crosby, extra engineer J.B. Bear and fireman Homer Eilertson. Eilertson lived in Vancouver on East Thirty-Ninth Street. They were traveling at about forty miles per hour as they crossed over East Reserve Street. Meanwhile, a freight train was heading onto a spur track at the Kaiser Shipyards. The last car on the train was a gondola car carrying great steel beams for the yards. The sound of the impact echoed across the barracks and the city. Crosby and Bears were crushed in the cab, and Eilertson was found dead under the baggage car.

Colonel Raymond Edwards, commanding officer at the barracks, hurried to the scene. Debris was scattered along the right of way. Motorists began to stop on the Evergreen Highway. Armed military police moved them on their way. Three soldiers suffered cuts and bruises, but fifty others were just shaken.

Perhaps what the security guard heard was the echo of the terrible sound of the train braking and the frantic effort of the train engineer to stop as he spied the gondola car blocking tracks.

THE WAYS

The huge concrete shipways that cradled the ships as they were built are still there. They're visible from a special-built Kaiser Tower just to the east of the former shipyards. Few people can go there because of the heavy industry all around. But those who have say that they have heard awful sounds coming from the ways, including moans and cries. That could be the strong wind that comes down from the Columbia Gorge and blows across the ways, but maybe not. Of all the many accidents that happened on the ways, most occurred when the ships were sliding down into the river. One was different.

Thirty-six-year-old Cliff Edward Knight was a maintenance worker in the yards. He and his coworker C.C. Burger ventured deep into the twists and turns of the shipyards. On April 24, 1944, a cloudy day with some showers, they descended into Way 11 to check pipes for leaks. There was a leak, and oxygen was whistling out of a pipe. There was a small fire nearby. The explosion wasn't large, as explosions go, but it was enough to immediately kill Knight. Burger was able to escape, although he was severely burned. Is that horrifying incident the cause of the eerie sounds that rise from the ways?

4
West Side Neighborhoods

Ruined by the Shipyards

Near Hough School is a small bungalow. You would not think it large enough to be divided into a duplex, but in wartime, anything is possible. Vancouver overflowed with newcomers. They had arrived to build the ships for victory. There was no place for them to live until the six wartime cities were built by the Vancouver Housing Authority. Many homeowners found that even the tiniest space in their house could be rented for a good sum, even a garage, an attic or the second-floor bedrooms. Into such a space moved a young family. The father, who worked at the shipyards; his wife; and three young children squeezed into the tiny rooms. One of the boys was in fragile health and spent most of his days in the children's hospital.

The good wages at the shipyard paid the bills, as did the revolutionary new concept of the Kaiser Company's health insurance. Things were different in Vancouver than on the farm in the South.

The end of the war was in sight, and the shipyards began to shut down. The father, along with thousands of others, faced unemployment. Maybe he had thought the high-paying days would never end. Who knows what went through his mind one warm spring evening.

The young mother napped on the couch. She awoke to a nightmare. Her husband towered above her, crashing an axe onto her again and again. She pled with him for her life. The terrified children cowered in their room,

An aerial view of Vancouver in the 1950s shows most of the Westside neighborhoods. The building in the center is the courthouse. *Author's collection.*

barricading the door as best as they could. Father crashed against the door, now armed with a .45 revolver. He threatened to kill them where they stood. He screamed that he was going to the hospital to kill the boy there. In a final eruption of rage, he raised the gun to his own head and pulled the trigger. The hysterical children bolted from the house and sprinted to the door of their neighbor.

The neighbor called the police, who made the gruesome discovery of the mutilated woman and the suicide. She whispered to the police, "He was a good man. The shipyards ruined him."

The house has returned to a single-family dwelling. Since that day, on the second floor and in the attic, residents have talked of sudden gusts of frigid air, whispers in the next room and soft moans. Old-timers on the street nod and whisper that it's the shipyard worker and his family reliving that awful night.

SEVENTEENTH STREET

Papers were the target in this house. There were papers that, if left on a table, would be on the floor with no draft of wind to blow them off. Every room in the house was subjected to the scattering. Then windows would rattle. Again, with no breeze to explain it.

The house had been damaged by fire. The way it burned is what gives the story. There had been prowlers and burglars infesting the neighborhood in warm August 1935. That night, a neighbor, Win A. Carson, called the police shortly after 2:00 a.m. to report that a wallet was taken from his clothing while he was sleeping. He had awakened to see a figure run from his house.

When the police responded, they saw the upper floor of the house on Seventeenth Street was ablaze. All of the doors to the house were unlatched. Dashing in, they found Irene and George Cate in one of the bedrooms, both dead. Irene had a wound to her head. George lay next to her.

The newspapers reported that they had both been killed by a burglar. The autopsies, though, told a different story. Irene had died from a blow to her head, but George had no wounds at all. He had taken poison and laid down beside his wife to die. First, though, he set three fires around the house. He set one upstairs, one in the kitchen and the third in the living room. There was money there and valuables that had not been touched. Completely burned were the financial records of a lodge, the Order of Red Men. George was the secretary of the lodge. Money had been embezzled from the lodge treasury.

The house was repaired, but few people would stay there for long. Eventually the house was torn down, and a duplex erected was on the site. It is hoped that George and Irene found peace once the house that held their downfall was demolished.

The House on West Nineteenth

There is a house on West Nineteenth Street in the Hough neighborhood that has a reputation for being haunted. It's a small, unadorned house with grey siding. There's a tiny porch and very little landscaping other than two evergreen bushes flanking the front walk.

The house was originally occupied by four French Canadian brothers, the Parmentiers, who came to work at the World War I Standifer Shipyards. They were painters, carpenters and laborers. It was probably not a sedate household with four young men in occupancy. In later years, tombstones were found under the house, probably stolen from the Old City Cemetery on Mill Plain. Neighbors assumed the brothers had taken them.

Later residents were plagued by small events. The water faucets would turn on unexpectedly and then turn off, as would the television set. Doors

On this street in the Hough neighborhood, a modest home has been the site of strange events for many years. *Author's collection.*

opened and closed by themselves. Perhaps the owners of the tombstones were trying to call attention to the theft, or perhaps it's a darker story.

Joseph Parmentier, one of the brothers who became a cook for the Forest Service after the war, shot and killed himself on March 29, 1948, in that house. No note was left and no indication of the dark pressures that drove him to that step.

One by one the remaining brothers moved on, but the spirit of Joseph, perhaps, remained behind.

OLD HOUSE RESTAURANT

Uptown Main Street is a prime example of development along a streetcar line. The line from the ferryboat to Sifton was completed in 1910 by the Vancouver Traction Company. Both businesses and homes went up along the line. One of those was the home of Jules Beauregard.

Bungalow homes were the latest style in elegant design, and Beauregard's home on Main at Twentieth was the first of that style built in Vancouver. Beauregard liked to impress, and that house was unlike anything that Vancouver had ever seen.

He was a southern gentleman from New Orleans and a successful businessman, but being a southerner in this very northern town and his business, that of a pawn shop and jewelry store owner, kept him from moving into the higher social order of the city. His shop, Beauregard and Beauregard, which he ran with his wife, Elizabeth, was at 702 Main Street. It was easy to hop on the streetcar and commute a few short blocks from home.

One afternoon a young man named Brent came into the museum with a story. He had grown up in the house after it became a rental. He'd always felt afraid there. Just inside the front door was a cold spot that was never warmed. Ornaments were tipped over, and dishes fell out of the cupboard. At night, he'd hear footsteps on the stairs. He'd seek the traditional haven of children and hide under the covers. That always worked. The steps would pause outside his door and then all would be peaceful again. His family moved on, and the house became a series of restaurants.

What had happened in that house, he asked, what terrible thing had caused those occurrences? Although it had been years since his family moved

The Craftsman-style home that Jules Beauregard built on Main Street was the first Craftsman built in Vancouver. It has been converted to restaurant use over the years. *Author's collection.*

away, his childhood memories were vivid. The story was easy to find. On a hot August afternoon in 1919, Elizabeth Beauregard took the streetcar to the jewelry shop. In the back office, she and her husband began to argue. He was preparing to go on a hunting trip.

She cried, "I know what kind of deer you'll be hunting for." She snatched up a revolver from the desk and shot him. She turned to a clerk, Edwin McLean, and said, "If he hadn't been so mean, I would never have shot him!"

McLean later testified that he blurted out that Jules had given her anything that she wanted. Sergeant Harry Burgy arrested her with the proverbial smoking gun in her hand. She originally pleaded temporary insanity but later withdrew.

Chief of Police Lee McCurdy read Beauregard's dying words to the jury at her trial: "I am going to die. I was going on a hunting trip, and she objected and grabbed the gun and shot me. I don't think she meant to shoot, she meant to scare me. The gun jumped from her hand when she shot. Let her go, Mac. Don't do anything to her."

Judge W.O. Chapman instructed the jury that they must find her guilty of first- or second-degree murder or find for acquittal. The dozen men on the jury found her to be not guilty. She was sent home to that house to live out her days, supporting herself with music lessons. She died on Christmas Eve in 1962 and was laid to rest next to her husband at Holy Cross Cemetery in Washougal.

Brent was satisfied. His sense that something awful had happened was vindicated. Yet there is another puzzle. What was the cause of the disturbances? Is it Jules in the house he loved, shot down in the prime of life? Or is it Elizabeth, spinning out her days in the home her husband built for her, always remembering what she'd done?

CORNER SHOP

Across the street from Carter Park, on the west side of town, there's a little shop. It is a cozy little building with white trim. It was at one time a pie shop. The owner of the pie shop, Marcell Garcis, had stories to tell. Things happen in that shop. One of the chefs had cooking utensils thrown at her. Waitstaff has seen a woman with her hair in a bun peeping through the windows into the patio seating. They can describe her: she has gray hair and is wearing a black dress with a white apron.

First built as a grocery store and residence by Lucius and Celia Bagley, the building has been used as a tavern and then a restaurant. *Author's collection.*

A section of the building was walled off at one point. There was a fireplace that was covered over with wallboard. Wiring was exposed. Eventually, a fire broke out that heavily damaged the building. During repair and remodeling, a wall was torn down, and the fireplace with a large mirror over it was revealed. The mirror was filthy from being walled up for many years. Marcella tried to clean it, but it required professional help. She hired a worker to clean it up.

He approached her that afternoon after he had finished. "You know that you have a ghost here," he said. "She said to tell you never cover up a mirror." Every employee had a story to tell, from pinches to taps to sounds. They agreed that it was a woman. They agreed that she did not care for men.

The shop has had many roles through the years as a tavern and coffee shop but primarily as a grocery store. The first grocery was built and operated by Lucius and Celia Bagley. Lucius had come to Vancouver to work for Charles Slocum, the builder of the Slocum House. Charles was a hostler, that is, he dealt in hard goods with the army. Junius was a driver for Slocum. He learned the retail business and eventually set out on his own.

Celia was the daughter of Irish immigrants and was born in Battle Ground. Celia didn't behave the way most young girls of her era did. She set off on her own at an early age. She moved into Vancouver, then to Portland and then back again to Vancouver.

In 1892, she married Lucius. They moved around from Vancouver to Seattle to Portland. They soon separated, and Celia began moving around. Every year she appears in different city directories at different addresses as a waitress and then as a maid at the Marion Hotel and then as a ticket agent at The Oks. Interestingly, she began to list herself as the widow of Lucius. The next year she was again Mrs. Bagley. Then in 1917, a legal notice appeared in the St. Helens newspaper stating that she was divorcing Lucius. The next year she was in Seattle with him, where he had bought a grocery. Then in the early 1930s, they were together in Vancouver. That is when he built the store that we see today.

In all subsequent records, they are together in the grocery store at the corner of Thirty-First and Columbia. Then on January 23, 1944, Lucius passed away. Celia lived on at the store until her death.

Rose Village Thing

Though perhaps not a ghost or a haunting, there is an otherworldly mystery, an unexplained event, that happened in Rose Village just after World War II. Just what was it that fell on Rose Village in 1946? Something came out of the sky with an intense light. It came straight down as if dropped. There was a meteor shower that night. The Giacobini-Zinner comet was going to pass overhead and treat the earth to a fiery display. The newspapers predicted the best show since 1909.

Ilia Cowie was a thirty-six-year-old nurse. She and her husband, Marshall Cowie, lived on Q Street near Fourth Plain. On October 19, she was driving west on Thirty-Third Street, taking her mother to the train station. Suddenly, the night lit up with a white glare.

Mrs. Robert Kadow, who lived at Thirty-Third and P Streets, said, "It lit up our dining room window, so I ran outside to see what it was."

Other witnesses said that "it fell straight down—a tremendously bright ball of light."

The thing came down at about M and Thirty-Third Streets. Ilia stopped her car and ran to where it had fallen. It was about the size of a baseball, and it was hot. The grass and weeds where it landed were burned about a foot around it. As she picked it up, it shattered.

The object was sent to the University of Oregon. There a geologist, Dr. Lloyd Staples, said that it wasn't a meteorite. "A meteorite," he said, "has iron and nickel. This specimen has neither."

It then was sent to another expert, Dr. J. Hugh Pruett, a meteorite expert. He agreed that it wasn't a meteorite. "A meteorite would have made a very loud noise. This was silent," he stated. "Meteorites don't burn white," he added. "It would have to have been traveling at forty-one miles per second to burn white. Meteorites in this cluster travel at only fourteen miles per second and burn red or yellow."

As unexplained as a haunting, though not a ghost, it is a spooky thing, nonetheless.

HIGH SCHOOL KILLER

Just off Main Street, in a quiet neighborhood, stands a modest home. It is an attractive house, and an average family lives there now. Odd things have been reported there over the years: a cold spot in the dining room and the sound of beads rolling across the dining room floor. Clearly something happened in the dining room. The rest of the house had no problems. A woman who had been a teenager when she lived in the house had a feeling of overwhelming sadness and loss in the dining room. Clearly, it was not a situation conducive to happy family meals.

Once again, the museum was contacted. This was easy to find because it was one of the most famous murders in Vancouver. In December 1946, a pretty high school girl, LaDonna Toscas, came to town to live with her father. He didn't have room for her, so she stayed with his business partner, Pete Tamis, until he could find a house for her. This wasn't easy to do in the '40s. The war was recently over, and there was a housing shortage because of all the returning veterans. It was Christmastime, as well, which is not an easy time for house hunting.

The young woman attracted the attention of a dark-haired boy, Joseph Maish, a star athlete at Vancouver High School and a friend of the business partner's son. He watched her and lusted for her. On a late December evening, she sat down to type some letters at a desk in the dining room. The young man stood and watched her and then wandered to Main Street. He stopped at the movie theater and talked to his friends. Among them was the business partner's son.

They talked and joked as young people do. The group went into the theater thinking that Maish was with them, but he wasn't. He'd lagged back. He went back to the house and called to the girl. She stood up and walked toward him in the kitchen. He grabbed for her. She struggled. Her pearl necklace broke, and the beads rolled across the floor. She screamed. He couldn't stand that, so he tried to quiet her. She screamed again. He grabbed a pastry knife and slashed at her throat. She struggled away, and he stabbed her again.

Joseph Maish was convicted of murder while still a teenager. His life was spared just sixty-six minutes before he was to be hanged. *Author's collection.*

Dying, she fled the house. He ran. LaDonna stumbled next door, where Gertrude Beedle opened the door to a horrifying sight. The gasping, bloody girl fell into Gertrude's arms. She died just inside her front door. The police were called, but the neighbors weren't sure who the young girl was. The bloody trail that she'd left was distinct. Next door they found the blood-spattered scene of the crime and pearls from her necklace scattered across the floor.

The young man who lived at the house was interviewed. His friends at the Mission Theater gave their stories. Joseph Maish gave himself up to the police. He did not know until then that LaDonna was dead.

The town reeled. These were not bad kids. The girl had been at home, safe and minding her own business. The other youngsters were just having a good time. The killer was a good student. He was quiet and the pride of Vancouver High's athletic department. How could this have happened here?

He went to trial in the spring, pleading insanity. It was pointed out that he liked to watch the young ladies at a dancing school practice and that he had a collection of *Esquire* magazines in his room. His own comment was that he'd been listening to too many radio programs.

He was sentenced to hang. The day of his execution arrived. He was dressed in execution garb: a shirt with no tie. For his last meal he asked for a cream puff. The guards brought him six. He waited and wept hysterically. Governor Mons Wallgren was uneasy at the idea of executing a seventeen-year-old boy. Sixty-six minutes before his execution, the governor called the warden and commuted his sentence to ninety-nine years.

In 1968, Governor Dan Evans granted him parole. He'd been a model prisoner and had obtained a college degree. He was freed. The tragedy was not healed by his conviction, and maybe the little house still feels the horror of that cold December night. Perhaps the young woman, still bewildered by what befell her, still sits typing her letters. Maybe one day she'll be at peace, and the sound of the little pearls rolling across the floor will be heard no more.

ARNADA'S CHEERFUL GUEST

There's a modest frame house on E Street in Arnada that has the kind of ghost that anyone would want, if one were to be haunted. The occupant knew that someone had been moving through the house, seen just out of the corner of the eye. When she'd turn, there would be nothing there. She could hear someone moving in another room, but when she would check, the room was empty. Once, a beam of sunlight shining through a bedroom window was cut as though someone had crossed in front of it. Yet she felt no threat or fear.

One afternoon a visitor stopped by. She walked through the house and into the kitchen. "Who's your gentleman friend?" she asked.

"What gentleman friend? I don't have a gentleman friend!"

"The man sitting in your living room. The one with one leg. He smiled and nodded at me as I passed him."

Both women hurried into the living room, but no one was there. The house was fairly easy to research, but the history of the former occupants was not. Surprisingly, for an older home, there had been few families who had lived there. One, who'd lived there the longest, had been a road master for the railroad before abruptly becoming an accountant. Had he lost a leg on the railroad? That was not an uncommon event in those days.

He seemed like such a nice man. They all agreed that he would be a welcome guest. So far, he's still there, sitting in the sunshine.

A FRIENDLY VISITOR

In the Lincoln neighborhood, near Lincoln School, is a cozy two-story home that dates to the late 1940s. The present owner has had several experiences with someone else who still lives there. While they watched one day, an unseen hand turned a vase of flowers so that a prettier view of the arrangement was revealed. "Yes," said the wife, "I like it better that way too."

As the man of the house worked at his computer, he sensed someone behind him, watching over his shoulder. He leaned back from his writing. "Is that OK?" he asked. Of course, there was no answer. No one was there. The family accepts that a gentle soul lives in the house with them. So, who could it be?

There was basically one family in the house for decades, Frank and Lucy. Frank was a barber, first working for other barbers and then owning his own shop. His wife, Lucy, was a housewife and church member. They built the house and lived in it together for almost ten years, until Frank died. Lucy lived on in the house alone for another thirty years. They were two gentle people who perhaps didn't want to leave their home. Maybe it is Lucy who still takes the time to rearrange the flowers for the new family. It also appears that she approves of them.

OUT OF THE SKY

On a corner at the southern edge of the Carter Park neighborhood, near Fourth Plain Road, stands a well-kept duplex. A tenant in one of the units came into the museum with an odd story. The building was relatively new, especially at that time. The person told me of a terrible cold spot in one of the bedrooms. Sometimes the room would be filled with the smell of smoke that was almost overpowering, and in a trice, it would be gone. She felt such a sense of impending doom while living there that she moved out.

She called the next tenant to see if she had had similar experiences, but she had not. The tenant in the other half of the duplex also had no problems. An overnight guest in the house, though, did smell the smoke and was quite alarmed. Once again, however, the smell dissipated as quickly as it had come.

There was a house on the property before the duplex was built, a two-story frame house. What had happened to it? Could a veteran firefighter remember a structure fire there in the 1970s? Oh, yes, he could, as a matter of fact. It was a terrible event.

On a Saturday in October 1977, a young wife was planning a celebration. An immigrant herself, she had just learned that her family had been granted

A Piper Navajo, similar to the one who came down in a Vancouver neighborhood with tragic consequences. *From a Piper Aircraft brochure collection of Ivan Bronson.*

permanent status. The family was gathering for a party. Taeko Halgren, just twenty-nine and the mother of two, was excitedly talking on the telephone with other members of her family in Japan. Each of her two children spoke to relatives and then she shooed them out of the room and sat on the bed to finish the conversation.

At Pearson Field, a 1971 Piper Navajo taxied down the field en route to British Columbia on business. Three men were on board. After takeoff, the plane began to falter. The pilot tried to turn it back toward Pearson, but he didn't have enough altitude to bank. He came in low over the shopping center at Kauffman and Fourth Plain.

A witness, Lorraine Fallein of Portland, was just unlocking a Goodwill box to gather the donations. She heard the plane flying very low. "It was having engine trouble and waving from side to side." She thought it was headed directly for her and began to run.

The plane leveled off and then turned on its side and crashed into the alley north of Fourth Plain and exploded. All three men on board were killed.

Fuel from the full gas tank exploded into flames, covering the side of the house. Taeko's sister ran into the house. She saw her sister standing on fire before she fell onto the bed and the flames roared up. Taeko's family stood on the sidewalk and watched as the house was totally consumed. The family sadly returned to Japan—their reason for staying had been taken away. Later, the duplex was built on the same site. Does the memory of that horror from a clear blue sky still remain?

COMMISSIONER

There is a little spot of green at Twenty-Eighth and K Streets called Leach Park. It's named for the first superintendent of Vancouver schools. It's a place for neighborhood children to play. Strange things have happened at this little oasis. Sometimes there is a foggy light that flickers here and there. Sometimes it is just above the sidewalk or in the park or just above the street pavement.

A neighbor, Mrs. Olsen, became worried about the light, thinking it was a gas leak or an electric discharge. Not too many neighbors were aware of it, and none were concerned. The city had no record of utilities there, nor did Northwest Natural. Well, maybe there was a prior use of the property that could account for it.

The land had been owned by the Hidden family until they donated it to the city for parkland. It stood empty for many years until the playground was built. A passing conversation with a member of the Hidden family pointed to a sad story.

The county was installing a sewer line down the street in 1940. F.W. Paul Schumann, the construction superintendent and a former Clark County commissioner, was inspecting the work. He went into the ditch and it suddenly collapsed around him. He was pinned against a concrete manhole. The workers tried to rescue him by drilling into the concrete walls of the manhole, but that didn't work. For several minutes, Schumann directed his own rescue but soon lapsed into unconsciousness. It took two hours to reach his body.

The street has changed greatly since 1940, but maybe the commissioner is still wandering about, checking the work or trying to figure out what the heck happened.

A PHANTOM CLOCK

Near Washington School is a house haunted by a clock. It is heard from time to time and sounds like an old pendulum clock. It ticks away the night hours, occasionally chiming. The present occupants don't own such a clock. The source of the sound cannot be located.

The house was owned by an ambitious young businessman during the Depression years. Times were hard. Even though he was from an old and well-known family, he and his brother had worked hard to make their business go. It is surprising just how achingly young these brothers were. When Herbert married his wife, Mildred, just three years earlier, he had to get his parents' permission to wed because he was just eighteen. His brother, Phil, was just two years older.

They ran a candy and tobacco business in Vancouver. They sold to small shops and stores. Herbert was a punctual man. His brother's widow, Flossie,

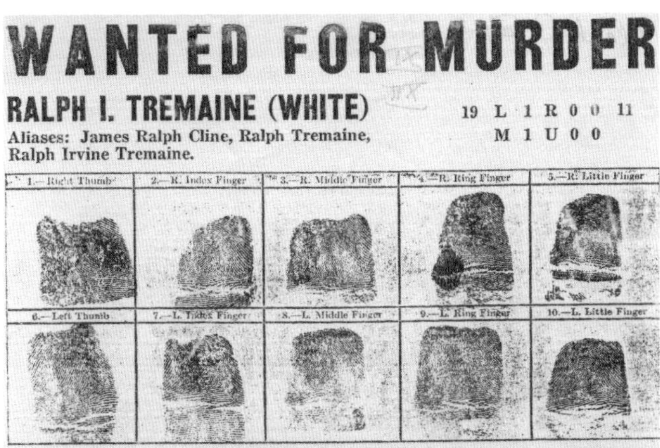

WANTED FOR MURDER

RALPH I. TREMAINE (WHITE)

19 L 1 R 0 0 11
M 1 U 0 0

Aliases: James Ralph Cline, Ralph Tremaine, Ralph Irvine Tremaine.

1.—Right Thumb	2.—R. Index Finger	3.—R. Middle Finger	4.—R. Ring Finger	5.—R. Little Finger
6.—Left Thumb	7.—L. Index Finger	8.—L. Middle Finger	9.—L. Ring Finger	10.—L. Little Finger

Age 23 yrs., 5 ft. 7½ in.; 160 lbs.; Hair, dark brown, wavy; Eyes, blue; Comp., dark. Marks Cic at cor. right eye. Jackson County, Oregon. #2166, Cincinnati, Ohio. PD #28333, Washington, D.C. #2268. Tremaine has a very close friend Leslie (Buck) Wilson (OSP #11495). Tremaine has admitted serving a term in the State Training School at Woodburn, Oregon. Has wife, Luella; no description, except she has auburn hair and very good looking.

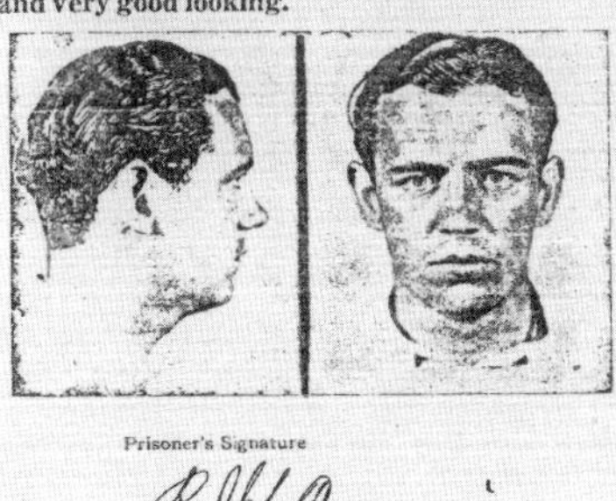

Prisoner's Signature

Ralph Tremaine

WANTED FOR MURDER of Herbert Caples, tobacco salesman in Vancouver, Washington, the night of March 10th, 1934. This man and his partner, Glenn Stringer, who has confessed his part in the crime, waited for Caples to return home on Saturday night after they had learned that he carried large sums of money, stuck him up, murdered him and robbed him of about $560.00.

If located, arrest; wire
Frank B. Osmond, Chief of Police
Vancouver, Washington.
or
Leland F. Morrow, Sheriff,
Clark County, Washington.

One of several wanted posters issued for Ralph Tremaine over the years. He was finally located decades later in a mental hospital. He was never charged. *Author's collection.*

once said that he was the sort of man you could set your watch by. He always left the house at the same time, always took the same route to work and always came home at the same time. He also collected the money due him at the same hour on the same day each week.

Someone noticed his routine. On that night, Herbert was going to vary his routine. There was a family party, and he was just going home to change clothes. Glenn Stringer and Ralph Tremaine saw the routine. Tremaine recruited Stringer for "easy money." They arrived at the house two hours ahead of Herbert's arrival. They broke in and stole an inexpensive watch. They were waiting for him to come home that cool March evening in 1934. As Herbert left his car, they announced their presence with revolvers. He quickly surrendered the cash and the cigarettes he had in his car. That did him no good at all. They shot him down and then shot him again in the head as he lay dying in the driveway. The pair fled into the night.

The murder has echoed through the years, affecting other members of the family. His brother, from that day forward, would not take the same route. He varied his hours and his paths. Perhaps the clock is reminding us all to do the same—to not get locked into a routine or maybe just that life is too short.

EERIE ROCK-AND-ROLL

On the edge of the Rose Village neighborhood, off SR 500, there's a little house that hides a tragic past. It once had a broad front yard where children played. The lawn has given way to street now, and the house doesn't have the cozy look it once had. Cars zip by going to and from the highway, never giving it a second glance. There's music in the house. It comes and goes. It's not quite identifiable, but it is music of another time. Music that would have been played on a 45-rpm record player.

In the 1960s, a divorced woman lived there with her three children. They were average kids, Bonnie, Freddie and Raena. They liked music and loved their mom. Their mom, Blanche, was adjusting to single life and was part of the active tavern life of Vancouver in that day.

In a tavern one night, she met a good-looking, though somewhat dangerous-looking man, John Hawkins. He was not tall, and he had thick, dark hair and tattoos on his forearms reading, "Death before Dishonor" and "Born to Lose." He had the air of a capable man.

He drove her home from the tavern one night and stayed on. He didn't seem to be able to hold a job, but he helped around the house and kept an eye on the kids while she worked. He slept on a settee, and Bonnie had a bedroom upstairs. One night they had an argument, and he moved out. Some weeks later, Blanche and the children wrote to him, asking him to come back. Now he and Blanche shared the upstairs room, and Bonnie and Freddie had a room in the basement. The children disliked that and began bickering about the arrangement.

One evening, Bonnie and Blanche went out. Hawkins didn't believe Blanche when she told him where she was going. He began to drink cough syrup called Tussar, an opioid-containing cough syrup that is strictly controlled. When he finished the bottle, he took yellow jackets (Nembutal). When that was gone, he took ampules of another medication that he couldn't name. He mixed it with cup after cup of coffee. When that was gone, he ate five peyote buttons. That's when he and Freddie began to bicker again. Freddie thought the living arrangements were ruining his mom's reputation. He slapped at Hawkins.

He did not know, nor did Blanche, that Hawkins was a violent man and that he was on parole. He had spent time in a mental institution. Now he was deep into a narcotic psychosis. When Freddie slapped at him, Hawkins picked up a hammer and began to beat him. When the child collapsed, he stabbed him to death. Then he sat and waited for Bonnie.

When she came in and saw Freddie, she screamed. Hawkins lunged at her and killed her the same way that he'd slaughtered her brother. Then he waited for Blanche. When she came home, he said, "The kids went to sleep right away. You'd better call the police." Then he ran. He stole a car down the street and headed for the Canadian border.

In the basement bedroom, she found her son and her daughter, beaten and stabbed to death.

Hawkins was captured at the Canadian border and returned to Vancouver. At the end of the trial, the jury found him not guilty of killing Freddie, by reason of insanity because of all of the drugs he'd taken. But they found him guilty of first-degree murder for the death of Bonnie.

He appealed, and during one of his appeals, he fashioned a handcuff key from a ballpoint pen cartridge and overpowered the two deputies bringing him back to Vancouver. He handcuffed them to a tree and stole the patrol car.

He was eventually recaptured, and his death sentence was reversed. He spent the rest of his life in prison. He never gave a reason for his horrendous act. No one can explain why some people do the things that they do. No one can explain the music, either, which should come from a 45-rpm player.

MUMMY OF LAVINA

"My neighbors have told me that something awful happened in my house, and I really would like to find out what it was." This is always the prelude to an interesting story and often some hard work. The woman on the telephone sounded reasonable. The discussion could have been about a book club or a council meeting, but it wasn't. She was positive that there was at least one and maybe two ghosts in her house. One, she was sure, was a female.

Household items were moved about. A paper holder from the bathroom would be found by the fireplace in the living room. Small objects would appear on the dining room table, carried from elsewhere in the house. She heard noises, thumps and rattles.

Then there was the water. Empty bowls in the dining room hutch would fill with water. The sheets on the bed would be wet—not the blankets, mind you, and not the spread on top, just the bottom sheet would have a little pool of water.

The little house sits back from the curb and is shaded by trees. It's a rather typical house for its era, the 1940s. A small porch leads to a door with a window in it. The fireplace is just inside. The house was built in 1943, during World War II. The owner was the district manager for the state tax commission, and the wife was listed as a housewife. They were ordinary folks. The wife died in 1957.

An out-of-the-ordinary thing showed up in the records then. A couple of no relation to the family moved in with the man. They were both hairdressers and owned a popular little shop in downtown Vancouver. Maybe the wife had been a client of the shop, and they moved in to care for him. They continued to live there and run the shop for another ten years. Maybe this is the cause of the water? A hairdresser would be around a lot of water. But maybe it's not.

When the old gentleman passed away, the hairdressers left to live in another house on the west side, and the little house was sold. Another childless couple moved in, Donald and Gwynn Layne. He was a saw filer (lots of water there) for a shingle mill. He loved to work on crossword puzzles and argue politics and was involved in the lumberman's union. He suffered from emphysema and took frequent naps. She was a housewife. They were not the sort of people who would be involved in a gothic tale.

One afternoon he stuck a newspaper clipping in his pocket. It was about an awards ceremony hosted by Trailblazer guard Clyde Drexler. Donald told his wife that he was going to take a short nap. He walked into the bedroom but never made it into bed. He died in the bedroom, on the floor, fully clothed.

Fast-forward to December 1993. Neighbors grew alarmed when they did not see Mrs. Layne out in the yard for several days. The tiny woman loved to work in her garden. They called the police and asked them to do a welfare check. Through the window, the police officer could see her on the floor. They broke in. She had fallen and could not roll over or stand.

It was a hoarder's house. Newspapers and magazines were stacked in high piles, forming passageways through the house. Since she stood just over four feet, the house was clear of cobwebs only to that level. Above that, they hung like stalactites throughout the house. She had been without food or water for several days. She had fallen on Saturday, and it was now Thursday afternoon. The paramedics arrived. They treated her and asked if she lived alone.

"No, my husband is here."

"How is he?" they asked.

"Oh, about the same," she replied. "He's in the bedroom."

In the bedroom, they discovered the gruesome sight of a mummified body. His pension checks were scattered through the house. His Social Security checks had been electronically deposited in his bank account. It became important to both the Pension Board and the Social Security Administration to discover when he had died so they could get the money back. The newspaper clipping in his pocket gave the probable date.

What made her keep her husband's remains in the house for a year?

Later she would tell doctors that when she found him dead, she simply didn't know what to do, so she covered him with a blanket and shut the door. Was she just not able to cope with the duties of funerals and death? Perhaps she chose not to believe that he had died. Maybe she was afraid to let anyone in the house. Whatever the reason, the neighbors still whisper about the mummy of Lavina.

When new occupants move in and find small objects moved about and bowls filled with water, they might ask if it is the little woman who was on the floor for several days without water. Or is it her husband, slowly dying on the floor of the bedroom.

THIRTY-EIGHTH STREET

It's a lovely house—the roof is steeply pitched with curved shingle edges and the inside has fine detailing. It's in a quiet neighborhood with well-kept homes and is walking distance to a grocery store. In the dining room are two built-in corner china hutches. In those shelves, small objects have been moved, and occasionally, one or two crash to the floor. While the doors don't open by themselves, doorknobs rattle with no hand to move them.

It was cloudy day on Saturday, April 28, 1978. Noma Simerly was at home alone. Her husband, Wallace, was out of town. She often left her doors unlocked during the day, especially if she was working in her yard. French doors led from the dining room to the back garden. Late April would be a good time for spring gardening. Perhaps that day the door was unlocked, or maybe she answered a knock at the front door.

A teenager, Michael Allen Hersh, burst into the home. The struggle must have lasted several minutes, and Norma was stabbed four times and bludgeoned with a length of firewood. Then all was still again.

Norma's mother found her body the next morning. A week later, in Hazel Dell, Hersh struck again. This time, however, the woman was able to escape.

A charming home in the Lincoln neighborhood once held a horrific scene. It seems to be quiet now. *Author's collection.*

She identified Michael, and he was arrested. Captain Robert King of the Vancouver Police Department later said that he was sure that Michael had killed Norma Simerly but could not prove it.

The years went by and then a decade, and another. The century changed, but Norma's murder was still listed as unsolved. Her parents died, and her husband moved on and eventually remarried. Norma's remains are at Evergreen Cemetery. In the meantime, DNA science developed and improved. Finally, thirty-three years and four months after the crime, Michael Allen Hersh was convicted of the murder of Normal Simerly with DNA evidence.

Perhaps now peace has come at last to the cottage on Thirty-Eighth Street.

PACKARD HOUSE

From Fruit Valley came tales of an axe murderer. "Oh, yes, a real axe murderer," they'd say owlishly. "A hobo came in off the railroad tracks and murdered those people in their beds."

There were no news headlines of such an event. It was an urban legend to be sure. However, there was a story that could have grown into the tale of an axe murder, as those tales do. The Packard House had a pair of gentle ghosts. They were nothing frightening, but objects moved, curtains were rearranged against the sun and doors slowly swung shut. There were some cold spots here and there about the house but never in the same places.

There had been a horrid event—a crime for which there was never a punishment, and it happened in the Packard House. The Packard House is a great old farmhouse built by Benjamin and Emma Packard in 1866. They were prune orchardists and businesspeople. It was added to the Historic Register in 1992. Benjamin and Emma left the house to relatives when they moved into Vancouver, and it was sold several times.

It was a cool and showery spring afternoon on May 2, 1963. It had been a dreary spring, and the newspaper reported that there had been no sunny days at all in April. Lyla Brasmer was going about her daily routine. She was probably having lunch. A dish of stewed tomatoes and a half-eaten sandwich was found in the kitchen.

Lyla was a well-known church worker and was active in the Emmanuel Baptist Church. She was about to start teaching a new class. There was probably a knock on the door or a sound from the porch, which was the start of terror. When Lyla opened the door, a man stood there. A description was

Lyla Brasmer was enjoying a peaceful lunch when terror knocked at her door. *Author's collection.*

given of a man seen in the area. He was a tall young man wearing a cap with ear flaps turned up and dungarees and was carrying a gray suitcase.

She was stabbed at the door, and a struggle began that carried through the house as her clothes were ripped from her body, and she was stabbed and stabbed again. When she stopped moving, he left the house.

After four o'clock that afternoon, Lyla's husband, Albert, came home from his work at Bemis Bag. He knew something was amiss when he saw mail in the mailbox. Once inside the door, he saw the evidence of a struggle and Lyla's garments strewn through the house. At last he found her body.

Police searched the "hobo camps" near the railroad. There was a parking lot for fishermen nearby, and they were questioned. A couple of men were picked up but released.

A few days later, Salem, Oregon police arrested a transient named Clifford Arthur Philips after he entered a Methodist church and caused a disturbance. He'd told police that he was staying at the Union Gospel Mission, but they quickly learned that wasn't true. They noticed that he resembled the description of the man seen near the Brasmer's farmhouse. He was wearing a fur-lined cap with ear flaps, as had been described. He had several silverware knives in his backpack. He had been a patient at Camp White Veteran's Hospital. That facility is now known as White City Rehabilitation Center and Clinics. He had been in prison in Minnesota for kidnapping and attempted murder.

Clark County said that they were no longer looking for that transient, and Clifford was just booked for vagrancy. No one was ever charged with Lyla's murder. Lyla was laid to rest at Evergreen Cemetery. Four months later, Albert was buried next to her. Friends said that he died of a broken heart.

Lyla's grandson, Randy, had a story of his own. He went back to the house as a young man, and it was boarded up. He pried the nails out of the plywood and entered. After wandering around the house, reliving old memories, he left. As he left, he put the nails back in the same holes to hold the plywood. When he returned a few weeks later, he saw that the nails were in place, but there was no evidence of tampering. He said, "I think my grandma was making sure that I didn't get in trouble."

Unander Street

Most Fruit Valley homes were built during the Second World War. Kaiser Shipyards had located in Vancouver, and the recently opened Alcoa plant was going full speed for the war effort. Thousands of workers streamed into the city, and housing was needed for them. The Vancouver Housing Authority was formed to build small cities connected to the city of Vancouver. One of the first of these was Fruit Valley. These first homes

The Fruit Valley neighborhood was one of the permanent homes built during World War II for the wartime workers at the shipyards and aluminum plant. *Vancouver Housing Authority collection.*

were solidly built with old-growth lumber. There was little variety in their façades or floorplans.

One of these, on Unander Street, was home to more than human occupants it seems. One former resident, Tara Lundy, described her experiences in the house. It began with her little girl, who would talk to an invisible person. She would tell her mother that she didn't want to play with that person anymore. In the evening, the little one would be put to bed, and the toys were put away in the toybox. Her parents would hear her talking and find the toys strewn across the floor.

They soon noticed that these things happened only when the child was in her bed. They set up an inflatable mattress on the floor, where the child slept undisturbed.

One night, Tara and her husband were awakened by the bed violently shaking. They sat up in bed and looked at each other. From the other bedroom, their daughter, who had crawled up into her regular bed, was crying out that her bed was shaking. The little family stayed up the rest of the night.

There was a window seat under the living room window, and on it, Tara had positioned a heavy vase full of pebbles to hold some large flowers. One morning the vase, flowers and pebbles were on the kitchen floor fifteen feet away. A fake fireplace that stood against the living room wall had been completely turned around.

At that point, they called in help. Tara contacted paranormal investigators, who told her that an early occupant was a man who was cheating on his wife. As she was at work and he was on the phone with his paramour, he neglected his little daughter. She fell and drowned in a kiddie pool. The investigators added that the mother committed suicide in her grief.

The hauntings continued after the investigation but were subdued. The Lundys sold the house and moved on.

THE DUPLEX

Elsewhere in Fruit Valley is a tidy little duplex. Next to it is Plum Village, a Vancouver Housing Authority development of quaint homes and apartments. Lights will turn on by themselves in the house, and sometimes a radio will do the same. It does not seem to stay rented for very long. There have been soft noises, as if objects are being pushed, yet nothing appears to have been moved.

Jack Taylor lived there with his wife, Jong Ja. They were both in their sixties. Jack had been a dockworker and recently retired. The marriage, however, had begun to collapse. Jong Ja told her husband that the marriage was over, and she would return to her native Korea without him. Her best friend, Joy Mei Shang Sun, joined her on a Saturday morning to help her finish packing.

Jack made one final plea to her, begging her to stay. When she refused, he pulled a gun and shot her, then Joy Mei Shang and then himself. Neighbors heard the women's screams piercing the morning calm. The police arrived at about 9:30 a.m. to find all three dead in the house. The next tenant was the first to hear noises in the afternoon. They were soft noises, as if objects were being pushed. It would seem that Jong Ja Taylor may still be trying to pack her things to leave.

MAUSOLEUM

Abandoned cemeteries would be bad enough, but to find out you've bought a house on the site of an abandoned mausoleum would give one pause. Yet that is exactly what happened to some folks in Edgewood.

It's a quiet, well-kept neighborhood not given to pranksters or vandals, but odd things happened. A garden hose placed out to water the lawn would be moved. Again, and again, the water hose would be in a different place than where the homeowner left it. He set out the hose and sat down behind the window to watch. The sprinkler chirped happily along. Nothing happened. The phone rang, and the gentleman looked away long enough to answer; when he looked back, the hose was moved. After a summer of brown spots on his lawn, the homeowner invested in an irrigation system, but the moving hose bothered him. He mentioned it to a neighbor one morning and found, to his surprise, that the same thing had been going on at the neighbor's house. Not only had his hose been moved but so had some of his patio furniture.

The story that they found answered their questions, but it was not one that they particularly liked. In the dark days of the Depression, in 1934, a group of businessmen gathered on a hillside off the Evergreen Highway. Just below

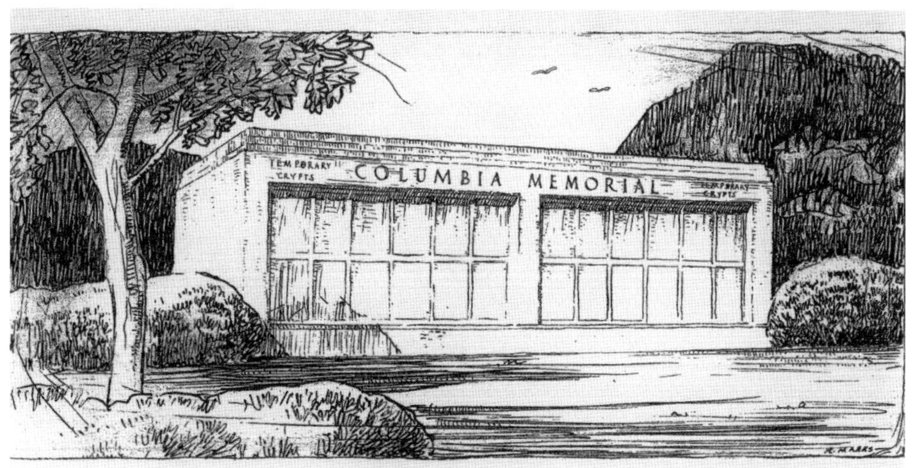

This drawing from a brochure for the mausoleum depicts the only structure ever built, the temporary crypts. *Clark County Historical Museum.*

the crest where Mill Plain runs, near Harney School, a grand ceremony took place. None other than Mayor John P. Kiggins turned the first shovelful of earth for the Columbia Memorial Mausoleum.

It was going to be a beautiful place. Great marble halls would be set off by the evergreen-covered hillside. Works of art would lead to contemplation by the mourners who visited their loved ones. A serene view of the Columbia River would be contemplated from marble benches. Shares were sold to the public, and money was raised. People died, and their remains were brought to be laid to rest.

A temporary mausoleum was built to hold the remains until the proper structure could be built. Three-foot tunnels were dug into the hillside. Unfortunately, times were hard, and money was scarce. The mausoleum was never built. The temporary structure began to crumble. Coffins were soon exposed to the elements. It was a gruesome sight, to be sure. Teenagers began to challenge one another to dare the exploration of the site on dark nights.

One night, three high school kids took one of the bodies. They put it in the back seat of their car and drove it to the Dairy Queen on Main Street. All they wanted to do was impress their friends and scare the girls. Too many people saw them, and the police were called.

They fled to the river and quickly slid the body into the water. It floated like a canoe. The police came to call. The boys quickly confessed, and they all eventually became respectable citizens of Vancouver.

It was admitted that the dream of the mausoleum was a failure. The bodies were removed and decently interred—most of them, that is. When the land was foreclosed on, most of the records of those interred were lost. A mother who reclaimed her teenage son's body opened the coffin and found a balding middle-aged man. Occasionally, more bodies would be found, and they were transferred to Park Hill Cemetery. The director of the cemetery, Bill McKechnie, can point to the area where all of the remains were buried.

After many years, homes were built up the side of the bluff. Tree-lined streets curve through the neighborhood. There are a few sunken places, but those prove to not be graves. People forgot the mausoleum, except maybe the former residents, who are reminding us of those days. Maybe they do it just by moving around a garden hose.

THRIFT SHOP

Very near Andresen and Fourth Plain is a commercial building that has seen many uses through the years. It began as a grocery store. For a few years it was a thrift store benefitting a local nonprofit. The clerks at the thrift shop were never quite sure what they would find in the morning. They knew one thing: the toys would be on the floor. There would be other things, including electronics that would suddenly stop working and electric lights that would go on and off. Once there was a radio that would go on by itself. There would be days when absolutely nothing would happen, but the toys would be on the floor.

On April 4, 1972, Vancouver experienced a thankfully rare occurrence. A tornado tore up the Columbia River, crossed it and bore down on the town. It came ashore at the site of the old shipyards and headed northwest. Churning across lettuce fields, it took aim at Peter Ogden Elementary School and flattened it within seconds. Next door, students at Fort Vancouver High School saw the destruction and, without prompting, dashed to begin pulling children from the wreckage.

The destruction was unfinished, and the cyclone next hit the Sunrise Bowling Alley. There was a housewives bowling league in progress. Some

The wreckage of the WareMart store after the tornado of 1972. Volunteers scrambled all along the path of the tornado to mount rescues. *Author's collection.*

of the women had brought their children with them and left them in the care of Sharon Graser in the nursery. The winds hit, a wall collapsed and Sharon Graser was killed instantly. None of the children were injured. The path of the storm crossed Andresen Road and bore down on the WareMart, a popular discount grocery and home goods store. Clifton Clevidence, just twenty-five then, was shopping with his wife, Luila; their five-year-old daughter, Denise; and their three-year-old son, Mike. Clifton was carrying his one-week-old baby, Mark. They were standing at the bread rack when the storm hit. The ceiling came down, knocking Mark from his father's arms and to the ground. Surviving from the family were only Clifton, with a fractured pelvis, and Mike. In an instant, a family had been destroyed. Elsewhere in the store, Jeannie Adams, with her two-year-old son, Brian Keith, heard shouts of alarm and ran toward the front entrance. Both were mowed down as the tornado moved on.

The destroyed Waremart would be rebuilt and, in time, would become Value Village, the thrift store. Could the mischievous ghosts in Value Village be the children taken so suddenly before they had a chance at life? Or could they be the mothers who lost the chance to play with their youngsters?

Toys would be easy to push off shelves if you wanted to make yourself known. Value village is closed, and the building has gone on to other uses. There aren't any toys there now.

MORRIS WOLF HOUSE

Morris Wolf was an exemplar of the American Dream. He arrived a penniless kid from the ghettos of Poland and grew into a successful businessman and entrepreneur in Vancouver. He built his stately home in 1935. The architect was Linn Forest, one of the architects who designed Timberline Lodge. He also designed the lighting fixtures for the interior. The house was considered to be so important that the *Columbian* newspaper devoted an entire page to it.

Morris sold the house to Bishop Lane Barton. He had been the prelate for the Eastern Oregon District of the Episcopal Church. When he retired, he and his wife moved to Vancouver. They called his wife Polly. Their children grew up successfully.

Polly grew too ill to climb the stairs to their bedroom. They made the dining room into a bedroom for her so that she'd still be part of the

The Morris Wolf House. The bay window on the right-hand side is the dining room where both Bishop Burton and his wife died. *Hovee family collection.*

family. From there, she directed the affairs of the house until she quietly passed away.

The bishop lived on in the house. His son bought the house across the street so that he could watch out for him. The bishop remarked that Polly would remind him to start the fire on cold mornings and to turn off lights left on too long. He was getting older, so no one commented. Then the bishop struggled with the stairs. Eventually, just as they had with Polly, the family made a bedroom in the dining room. There, as had Polly, the bishop quietly died.

The house was sold to a young businessman, Erik Hovee, and his wife, Beth. They moved in with their family. But Polly continued to supervise. The fires would be lit on a cold morning, and lights were turned on and off. Their daughters would, on occasion, see Polly moving down the halls of the house, still supervising.

That family grew up, and the house was sold. The tradition of the bishop and of Morris Wolf was passed on. On the wall is the framed copy of the full-page newspaper article marking the building of the house. We have not heard if Polly is still assisting in the management of the house.

Lost Cemetery

Close to the Washington State School for the Deaf is a row of apartments. A resident of one of them complained of sounds, creaks and strange lights in his apartment. He was sure that there were mice but attempts to capture the critters were unsuccessful, even as the skittering sounds continued.

The units were just a few years old. Since it was so new, the old Polk directories were checked, and nothing was found. However, a couple of weeks later, a patron came into the museum to share an old Vancouver newspaper that she had found behind a picture she bought at an auction. Ta-da! There, big as life, on the front page was a story. In 1935, while excavating for a new house, a graveyard was uncovered. Two skeletons in coffins of hewn cedar planks were found. One was a woman of about thirty years and the other was a man about six feet tall. Both had perfect teeth, it was noted. No clothing or any other objects were found in the coffins. It turns out that another skeleton, also in a coffin, had been dug up in 1933 in the Kampe gravel pit, just below East Fifth Street, about one hundred yards from this discovery. It has been assumed that the bodies were from the Hudson's Bay Company, since the original site of the company was on that bluff just east of the grave sites.

Well, well, it was an abandoned cemetery. The address was checked in the city directories, but no one was ever listed as living at that address. Did they not finish the house that they were building when the graves were found? Did no one live in the house long enough to be listed in the directory? That part of the story hasn't yet been discovered, but there was a reason for the tenant's experience. He still lives there, by the way.

5

East Side Neighborhoods

Lived Too Long

Awful things had been going on in the house, one of hundreds of 1970s ranch-style houses linked across the farmland east of the city. There were animal tracks going up the wall and across pictures and photographs hanging there. A closet, locked with a hook-and-eye fastener, had been thrown open, ripping the hook and eye from the doorjamb. Objects crashed onto the floor. The occurrences had begun suddenly, without warning.

Aerial photos from 1937 and 1945 showed farms and orchards, one after another. It's difficult to locate a neighborhood of today on those old photos. There are some of the old roads still, of course, and creeks and rivers haven't changed much. By comparing them with a current map, you can zero in pretty closely.

There was a little farm there, just ten acres, which was unusual for the area that had very large properties. The area then was called Burton, not to be confused with today's Burton neighborhood. Burton was a voting district and lay south of the Sifton District, all the way to the Columbia River.

What happened on a small farm in the Burton District? An old man was afraid, that's a matter of record. The night before he disappeared, he'd told a neighbor that he was afraid to go home. He'd been beaten and abused there and lived in fear.

He hadn't always been afraid. He hadn't always been old, either, but he was now. He was ninety-five years old, living alone in a tidy little house on ten acres. Louis D. Boucher was his name.

Louis Boucher was a rugged outdoorsman who lived on the trails in his beloved Grand Canyon. He met his end in Vancouver. *Author's collection.*

He led an adventurous life before coming here. He told neighbors that he'd once owned a copper mine in the Southwest. Not only that, he owned a scenic trail in the Grand Canyon, called the Boucher Trail. To this day, in the Grand Canyon there is the Hermit Road, on the west rim of the canyon. The hermit was Louis Boucher. He lived alone but was not a hermit, having an active social life in the spa area. He'd arrived in Arizona in 1891 and had invested in lands and properties nearby.

He kept the titles to those properties near him. He showed them to people, friends, acquaintances and neighbors. Everyone knew about them. Now he knew he'd never work the mine and never lead tourists down the trail. He was reaching the end of his life, though he was healthy and fit. He came to Clark County. He wanted to be near his sister, who had taken the vows to religious life with the Sisters of Providence and was living at Providence Academy in Vancouver.

To ensure his own well-being, he deeded the title to his farm to one Leon Jones, on the condition that he be allowed to live in his neat little house for the rest of his life, and Jones would take care of the farm, keep up taxes and generally see to the business.

The years passed. Jones tired of the bargain and sold the land and the bargain to Fred Jones (no relation). Fred saw a golden opportunity. After all,

Louis was a very old man. He was toothless and walked with the aid of a cane. But more time passed. Fred grew impatient almost immediately. Why wouldn't the old man just die?

He harangued the old man. Louis said that he abused him and struck him. Boucher filed a lawsuit in April 1935. He asked that the title be returned to him. He argued that Leon Jones shouldn't have sold the property. He said that the agreement had not given Jones the right to sell. He also swore that Fred Jones had not kept up the farm and hadn't paid the taxes. He charged the abuse. They were going to go to court in August. That suit was never to be heard.

On June 18, 1935, Fred reported to the sheriff that poor old Louis had gone missing. Probably senile, you know, he just wandered off. Nonsense, said the neighbors, he was as sound in mind as a twenty-year-old. They were sure that there was foul play. The neighbors helped search the surrounding farms for any sign of Louis.

It was foul play indeed, for on July 6, Boucher's body came floating to the surface of the Columbia River twelve miles downstream from Vancouver. A three-strand rope, cut from his own clothesline, had been knotted around his neck. The rope, thirty-five to forty inches long, had a neat knot also tied in each end so that it wouldn't slip through the murderer's hand should the old man struggle.

The crime scene was reconstructed. It seemed that Boucher slept in a straight-backed wooden chair. He was probably dozing, they said, when the culprit crept up behind him, looped the garrote around his neck and pulled it tight. It was done so quickly that Boucher's flowing white beard was tangled up in the rope. The old man's fear had been justified. That was the only justice he would get.

Fred Jones was arrested and charged on July 18. They charged that he had been the only one with a motive, opportunity and means to kill. They charged that after Louis was dead, Jones had driven his car, with the body in it, to the landing at Ellsworth and had thrown the body into the river.

On Halloween, Fred went to trial. The defense moved for dismissal on the grounds that the trial did not start before the statutory limit. October 18 was the last day that trial could have begun under the law, they said. The judge dismissed the case, and Fred Jones walked out of the courtroom a free man. We tend to think that legal technicalities are a modern-day occurrence, but here we see that no one was ever punished for the cruel death of the old man.

Several years later, just at the onset of World War II, a warrant was issued against a Fred Jones for child molesting, but he left the county, and the warrant was eventually canceled. Perhaps he went to the old man's copper mine, which he now owned, or maybe he wound up running tourists down the scenic trail in the Grand Canyon.

Ninety-five years on this earth, and Louis wasn't even allowed to die in dignity. Perhaps that is the reason for the explosion of anger in the house fifty years later

WOODS HOUSE

The most widely talked about haunting is that of the Woods House on East Thirty-Seventh Street. The Woods no longer live there but that's the name it will always bear. It's been written up in newspapers, featured in *Fate Magazine* and has been a segment on *Unsolved Mysteries* and *Larry King Live*.

Ed and Mary Wood reported that they moved into their ranch-style house on Northeast Thirty-Seventh Street in Vancouver in 1994. It's almost the epitome of a Vancouver ranch, with an attached garage that has since been converted, a front door flanked on one side by a large living room window and three smaller bedroom windows on the other. It has the typical gable

The Woods House, the most famous haunted house in the city. Its story has been told on television programs and in magazines. *Author's collection.*

roof with a brick chimney poking up in the middle. There is nothing to distinguish it from most other homes of the era. It's in the center of a cul-de-sac with similar homes.

Early events that the Woods noticed were the doorknobs rattling. Ed Woods thought it was his daughter playing tricks. He thought that he'd catch her in the act. He threw open the door, and there was no one there. Then footsteps were heard in the hall. Soon pictures on the wall would be rearranged and even carefully laid on the floor.

Mary frequently heard the sound of a music box being played. She often saw the figure of a nightgown-clad woman who seemed to have a scarf wrapped around her head. Other figures were of a man dressed as a gambler would dress, in a white shirt with a string tie. There was a small girl in a pink dress who the family called "Pinky" because of her dress. There was yet another shade that lurked in a shower and touched members of the family who were showering. In fact, that small bathroom seemed to be particularly haunted. It was always cold, and Ed Woods said that he couldn't sleep if the door to the bathroom was open. Once he did that, he said, and awoke to an entity sitting on his chest.

Psychics visited, and a paranormal researcher set up a crew there and wrote the events in *Fate Magazine*. The Woods could not explain why their house was so affected. Mary did find that a former resident had died in the house after suffering from a long battle with cancer. She believes that would explain the woman with the nightgown and the scarf. The Woods sold the house in 2005. The current owners have had no similar experiences

NINETY-EIGHTH AVENUE

On Southeast Ninety-Eighth Street, on the border between the Vancouver Heights neighborhood and the Ellsworth Springs neighborhood and smack in the middle of a 1960s development is a house with some lively spiritual activity. It's a one-story brick ranch, nothing about it looks at all spooky and the spirits in it are anything but spooky.

There is a man who runs across the backyard, of course, ignoring hedges, plants and fences. Then there is the shade that the family calls the Angry Man. He moves in the living room from the fireplace to the front door, sometimes slamming the door. The adorable spook is a long-haired gray cat. The other five cats often notice him first. They watch him cross the

It looks like many Vancouver ranch-style homes. Within, the family lives happily with several spirits. *Author's collection.*

room. Five cats watch the invisible cat in unison. The owners have seen his paw coming out from under the couch. Sometimes there is just a glimpse of him turning a corner. The home's owner, Lynnette Blackard, says, "He is a welcome visitor, always." The house across the street welcomed the ghost cat as well. They felt him jump onto their bed and curl up next to them.

Then there is a constant presence. That is Lynnette Blackard's father, Richard Reay. Richard was a longtime volunteer at the Historical Museum and with the Oregon Archaeological Society. He told his friends that he would be haunting the house. It seems that he is a spirit of his word.

Lynette told the story so well that I will simply quote her:

> *He passed away in the house. He has expressed himself quite well. At first, he could be seen sitting at the kitchen table, drumming his fingers.... He hasn't been seen at the table for a few years. We still see him passing by into the kitchen. And he finds my friend Vicky very pretty. He tries to contact her—touch her hair when she visits. Father was a watt watcher, a penny pincher. A Scottish family trait. Conservation of resources and lack of waste was important to him. He doesn't like the fact that I don't like the dark. I have dim lighting throughout the house at night. One particular*

light, a touch lamp, with a dimmer to off switch, is regularly turned all the way down in the morning but never clicked off, only dimmed, appearing off. I know *that's my father! He really didn't want us taking over the master bedroom. We slept on the couches for years. He has accepted us having the master bedroom. But I know one thing that won't* ever *change. He is going to dim the touch light for as long as it is left on at night in his house!*

FISHER HOUSE

On the old Evergreen Highway, near 164th Street, a house sits back from the road. It looks like it was built in the 1970s, but it is much, much older than that. It's the Fisher house of Fisher's Landing. The owner who reported this story was as hardheaded and practical a man as you could find. A graduate of the United States Naval Academy before World War II and a retiree from Bonneville Power, this is not a person you would say is given to flights of fancy. While discussing another interesting ghost story, he said, matter-of-factly, "My house is haunted too."

Well, that was like hearing him say, "Oh yes, I'm flying to the moon this evening."

Pressed for details, he talked of cold spots and noises. Sometimes, while working in his office, there would come a blast of cold air. The ghost doesn't bother him, and he doesn't bother the ghost. He figures the ghost liked the house so much that he still lives there. So, who could it be?

Let's look at the Fisher family. The whole family came from West Virginia in 1851. Making the long, six-month trip were Solomon, Job, Adam and Michael. Adam met and married an Oregon girl and settled across the river.

Job and Solomon settled on the north side. Solomon took out a land claim and built a dock. Steamboats were just about the only good transportation in the area. The roads were just trails, and there was no railroad. If you wanted to get your crops to market, you needed a landing. There were dozens of landings along the river. Most were mud landings. The steamboat simply nosed into the mud and threw out a plank gangway. What made Fisher's Landing unique was not only that Solomon had built a proper dock but that he and Job opened a store and a post office, which he called Fisher.

The store made a good gathering place. Soon farmers from the North began making their way there. They could ship their goods, stock up, gossip and check the mail all in one place. Their wagons cut a rut down to the landing that became a trail, which became a road that we now call 164th Street.

Job had a claim but failed to complete it, and it was canceled. When he was fifty-four, he married for the first time, a widow with three children. They had two of their own, Edna and Solomon Welton. Job and Solomon's store prospered, and the landing grew into a community.

Solomon died a bachelor in 1903. He worked almost to his last day. Job passed away in February 1905. In late July of the same year, it was hot. Edna Fisher and two of her friends tried to swim to Government Island. They never made it. All three girls drowned in the river. That left only Job's son, young Solomon Welton, to carry on the business.

When World War II came along, he went to work in the Kaiser Shipyards. On the May 20, 1944, a ship was being launched. The way they launched ships at the yard was to cut the great beams loose that had held the ship in the ways. The ship would slide backward into the river. As the great ship began to move, one of the beams skittered sideways, and Solomon Welton lost his footing and fell. He died instantly.

There were no more Fishers here. The house was sold. The owner thinks that it is Solomon Welton, Job's son, who is still in the house, perhaps not knowing that he's dead. It could be Edna, too, back from her swim. Or maybe old Solomon is still running the store and the post office, too busy to marry or do anything but work.

BLAIR HOUSE

Mattison and Lucinda Blair's house is not where it started, but then again, neither are its ghosts. The house was moved from its original site at 164th and Mill Plain to Northeast 39th Street. A new family bought the grand old house and lovingly restored it to the splendor it once had. The house was moved, and the ghosts moved along with it.

Mattison Blair came to Clark County from Missouri, found a job and worked to bring his family out West to be with him. He was a hardworking man—the very model of a pioneer. His photograph shows a husky man with thick dark hair and smile lines showing around a luxuriant moustache. Lucinda gazes at the camera, dark hair in a sensible style, with a hint of a ribbon in the back. Together they would have ten children.

Fisher's Landing, the store and the post office were just down the road from the Blairs' place, so it was a good place for a prune dryer. Fruit from the orchards around the plain could be processed there and could easily go

The Blair House, a historic farmhouse, was moved from its original location on Mill Plain Road west of 164th Street in 1969. *Clark County Historic Preservation Commission.*

to the landing to be shipped out on one of the paddle wheel steamers that plied the river.

Recognized as a hard worker, he was asked to become more involved in the tiny community. He served on the school board, and when space was needed to build Union High School, he donated the land. Mill Plain Elementary stands there now. He was the president of the East Mill Plain Telephone Company, one of many such systems that began the growth of communications. He died in 1934, and Lucinda lived on until 1949. They're both buried at the Fisher's Cemetery. They are hardly the type of family to produce a haunt.

Repugnant smells would arise in one section of the house. Someone would make noises at the door, but no one was there. An older woman was awakened one night and saw the form of a young boy. She ran out of the house. The present owner glanced at the television set, which was off, and saw the reflection of a young boy.

There was a young boy who was lost. Lauren Blair was only eight years old when he fell off a gravel wagon in front of the house in 1906. The wagon ran over him. His parents carried his broken body into the house. There was nothing to be done, and as they carried him through the door, his last breath left his body. His family buried him at Fisher's Cemetery, where they all rest together now.

The new family had the house blessed, and Lauren has not been seen since.

THE CENSUS TAKER

West of Lieser Road is a tidy, well-maintained neighborhood of middle-class homes. It is unique in that many of the houses are built of cinder block, an unusual building material in Vancouver. All of the streets are named for mountains in the Cascades. You would guess that the worst disturbance would be a leaf blower on a Saturday morning.

A young family moved into one of the houses and began making it their home. Disconcerting things began to happen. As they watched television one night, the front doorknob began to violently shake and twist. No one was there. One of the children asked their mother who it was that had been weeping in the night. No one had wept.

While working in the garden, a neighbor stopped by, and, as neighbors like to do, told her the ghastly story of her new home. Hulda Trautman was a plain little thing, a fifty-ish widow devoted to her Lutheran Church. She had worked for the church in Portland, taking a census of the parishes around each church and determining the religious connections of the neighbors. She was so thorough and conscientious that she was recommended to the Vancouver organization as well.

On a May morning in 1961, she set off walking door to door. In mid-afternoon, she reached the door of Owen Shook's home. Mrs. Shook's son, Donald Pribberow, was alone in the house. He'd recently arrived from California, where he'd been unable to keep a job. He had the same problem in Vancouver, drifting jobless with a string of petty offenses on his record. He was a lonely man with no friends. He opened the door to Hulda and invited her in.

Mrs. Shook arrived home that evening to a gruesome sight. Gouts of blood splattered the walls of her living room. More blood had sprayed across the dining room table. The carpeting was sodden with yet more blood. She was certain that something terrible must have happened to her son, Donald. His car was gone. She called the police. She gave them the license number to Donald's car. Later that night, a sheriff's deputy spotted the car in Hazel Dell. Pribberow ran. The police chased him. He headed for home. The quiet suburban street filled with police cars, sirens and flashing lights. In the house, Vancouver Police captain Eugene White was waiting. Donald surrendered.

He'd been lonely, he said, and had wanted someone to talk to. But then "she started talking religion," he exclaimed. He beat her with a baseball bat as she ran for the door, trying to escape. He stabbed her then, several times and strangled her. When she was dead, he put her body in his car and drove east. North of Camas, he dumped her body. He took the police to her body, dumped off a country road near the Livingston Rock Crusher. His trial was short. A psychiatrist declared him psychotic, and the jury agreed. Judge Eugene Cushing sentenced him to life without parole. He died in prison in 2002.

The young housewife became more and more shaken as the neighbor spun out the story. She was in tears when her husband came home. They called a minister and had the house blessed. Calm descended on the home. Hulda had not had the comfort of a pastor with her in her final hours, and it appeared that the blessing years later was all that she needed.

GLENN JACKSON BRIDGE

These stories began with the Interstate Bridge. It seems fitting that they should end with the eastern bridge, the I-205, named the Glenn Jackson Bridge. It's a modern soaring bridge across the Columbia, curving from East Vancouver over Government Island and landing on the Oregon Shore just east of the Portland International Airport. It is not a likely spot for a phantom.

Several times, motorists have been alarmed by the sight of a person sitting on the barrier at the side of the bridge, back to traffic, looking down at the river as if to jump. Then there is nothing. Emergency services are called. Nothing and no one are found. How could the figure have disappeared so quickly?

The Columbia and Willamette River systems often lead the nation in the statistics of drowning victims. Unfortunately, many are suicides off our several bridges.

Emergency services first go on the bridge to look for shoes. It seems that more often than not, suicide victims take off their shoes before they jump. When the shoes are found, an *X* is spray painted where they are found, and a plumb line is dropped at that point. The search begins at a radius around

The Glenn Jackson Bridge, the I-205, was opened on December 15, 1982. It is 11,750 feet long and has a 144-foot clearance. The opening changed Clark County forever. *Author's collection.*

the point where the plumb line meets the water. The river looks calm and placid. That is deceptive. It is a raging, rapid current. Sometimes the victim is never found. The last time emergency crews responded to the call of a young woman on the bridge, a faded *X* was all that was found.

Between the two bridges and beyond, a thriving modern city stands—ships on the river, planes in the air, traffic humming at all hours of the day. Where we pass, heedless, people before us lived and died, loved and hated, succeeded and failed. That makes up life and history.

BIBLIOGRAPHY

Newspapers

Capitol Journal
Daily Columbian, afternoon and morning editions
Longview Daily News
Medford Tribune
Oregonian
Statesman
Vancouver Independent
Weekly Columbian

Books

Clark County Genealogical Society. *Clark County Pioneers: A Centennial Salute.* Vancouver, WA: Clark County Genealogical Society, 1989.

Field, Pearson, and Bill Alley. *Images of Aviation.* Charleston, SC: Arcadia Publishing, 2006.

Harshman, Rose Marie. *Clark County Pioneers: Through the Turn of the Century.* Vancouver, WA: Clark County Genealogical Society, 1993.

Landerholm, Carl. *Vancouver Area Chronology.* Vancouver, WA: Fort Vancouver Historical Society, 1965.

Mack, Lois. *One Place Across Time.* Vancouver, WA: Vancouver National Historic Reserve Trust, 1999.

Sully, Langdon. *No Tears for the General.* Palo Alto, CA: American West Publishing, 1974.

Van Arsdol, Ted. *Northwest Bastion: The U.S. Army Barracks at Vancouver.* Vancouver, WA: Heritage Trust of Vancouver, 1991.

Miscellaneous

Fate Magazine, October 1998.

Grafton, Richard. "Vancouver Police, the Good, Bad and Indifferent 1855–2004. Unpublished manuscript, 2004.

Oral History Florine DuFresne. Center for Columbia River History. April 11, 2001.

Polk's Vancouver Washington City Directories

Unsolved Mysteries. Season 10, episode 4, "Haunting on 37th Street." Aired April 17, 1998, on CBS.

About the Author

Pat Jollota and her late husband retired together from the Los Angeles Police Department, where she was a civilian employee. They had long planned to move to Vancouver, Washington, where Pat could pursue a second career in historic preservation. That had to wait for a year, though, as they took on managing a three-hundred-year-old hotel in the Berkshires, United Kingdom.

Once back in Vancouver, Pat almost immediately became a curator with U.S. Grant House Museum and then the Clark County Historical Museum. She continued in that capacity for twenty-two years, absorbing the rich, overlapping, maddening history of Clark County. While there, she began her collection of historic photos and postcards of Clark County, many of which appear in this book.

Simultaneously, she was elected to the Vancouver City Council and served on the board for twenty years. This position enabled service on many other boards and commissions, some of which still continue.

This is her second book with The History Press and follows four with Arcadia Publishing. Before that, she published three with the Clark County Historical Society.